the *Southern* cosmopolitan

Sophisticated Southern Style

Susan Sully

RIZZOLI
NEW YORK

FRONT COVER Decorated by New
Orleans-based interior designer Hal
Williamson, this intimate sitting room
overlooks the courtyard of Debra and
Jerry Shriver's New Orleans townhouse. Indirect light illuminates the
brightly colored interior that includes
an Oushak carpet, Ikat-style upholstery on Louis XV chairs, and throw
pillows covered with opulent damask
by Silkworks Textiles®.

BACK COVER AND PAGE 1 A magnolia
bloom's porcelain-like petals capture
the late afternoon light in a townhouse
in New Orleans' French Quarter. The
Louis XVI chair is upholstered with a
contemporary toile pattern designed
by Roulhac Toledano after antique
maps and motifs associated with New
Orleans and Louisiana.

PAGE 2 Christa of Palm Beach, a
decorative artist specializing in shell
art, created this classical bust encrust-
ed with shells of every color and shape
imaginable. The large shells decorated
with silver were used in India as horns
to call the faithful to prayer.

OPPOSITE A replica of a 1910 Krewe
of Rex carnival crown, made by Cody
Foster, sits atop the original rouge
marble top of a French rococo desk in
the Shrivers' New Orleans pied-à-terre.

FIRST PUBLISHED IN THE UNITED STATES OF AMERICA IN 2009
by Rizzoli International Publications, Inc.
300 Park Avenue South
New York, New York 10010
www.rizzoliusa.com

Text and photography copyright ©2009 Susan Sully
except jacket flap and pages 8 ©Graciela Cattarossi; 159 ©Mick Hales; 160–61,
164, 166, 167 ©Gordon Beall; 162, 163, 165 ©Dan Bibb; 199, 201, 202–3
©Wayne Moore; endpapers: Silkworks Textiles®

2009 2010 2011 2012 / 10 9 8 7 6 5 4 3 2 1

Printed in China

ISBN 13: 978-0-8478-3078-7

Library of Congress Control Number: 2008943098

Project Editor: Sandra Gilbert
Designed by Element Group

Credits: On the endpapers, an over-scaled foliated pattern with soft edges and
antiqued patina designed and produced by Silkworks Textiles® captures the New
World, Old World, and global exoticism of the cosmopolitan South.

To the first Southern cosmopolitans who, despite all the challenges of seventeenth- and eighteenth-century living, created a tradition of extraordinary style.

Contents

Prologue

As a chronicler of Southern style, I have encountered elegant houses in Charleston and Savannah, exotic Creole dwellings in New Orleans, and chic urban rooms created by the region's top interior designers and architects. In the process, I have discovered a wonderfully fluid relationship between the past and the present in the South. For example, the Classical styles that were the hottest thing going in the eighteenth and nineteenth centuries are big all over again. The old is the new new, so to speak, in suburbs like Atlanta's Buckhead and Nashville's Bellemeade, where just built neo-Colonial Revival houses stand next to those built in the 1920s and 30s, when the Colonial Revival was also the style-du-jour.

Susan Sully sits amid European art deco furnishings and accessories in Carlton Dailey Twentieth Century—a shop located on King Street in Charleston, South Carolina, that epitomizes Southern cosmopolitan style.

The same pattern occurs in interior design, where the decorating details in vogue during the Georgian and Federal eras are popular once again. If you look at the covers of today's style magazines, you'll see faux-bois paint treatments, scenic wallpaper, and saturated colors like vermilion and turquoise. These same elements were embraced two centuries ago by Southern fashionistas living on the cutting edge of transatlantic style. Whether one considers these aesthetic antecedents to be accurate forecasters or today's design experts to be creative recyclers—the simple truth is that Southern style contains the past, present, and future all at once.

Another thing I noticed about Southern style is the intimate relationship between the local and the global. When you look at a Federal mansion in Natchez, for example, you are also seeing glimpses of England, Italy, and Greece. Take a peek inside, and you'll witness an interior that seems at first oh-so-Southern, but upon closer inspection is quite international, thanks to its English antiques, French chandeliers, and Asian textiles. Then consider an interior in Atlanta that appears to be a contemporary departure from Southern style, with Ming dynasty *huang-huali* chairs, silk sari curtains, and Afghanistani carpets. But if you remember that exotic accoutrements reflecting Asian influences were also status symbols in early Southern homes, it becomes evident that Southern style has always been geographically inclusive.

This South, which is both timely *and* timeless, local *and* global, is the place I celebrate in my books. In these pages, I present a group of design professionals and homeowners I've come to call "Southern Cosmopolitans" because they personify these attributes. Comfortable with trend and tradition, at ease with both the foreign and the familiar, they are urbane, au courant, and well versed in aesthetic history. When it came to choosing houses, I selected dwellings in cities that were active points of trade with foreign countries or other parts of the nation. Because trade builds wealth and stimulates awareness of fashion, houses in these locations have long been among the most sophisticated in the region. I wish I could have included many more people and places in this volume, and can only hope that I may have the chance to do so in my next.

Introduction

Moonlight and Magnolias, Revisited

Paintings of saints from an Italian church cover doors flanking the mantel in the master bedroom of Atlanta-based architect Norman Askins and his wife Joane, an interior decorator. Antique French chairs for children hold books about art, architecture, and the decorative arts.

When people think of the South, they conjure up images of moonlight and magnolias, white columns and wide porches, old chintz and Chippendale furniture. No matter how cliché, these romantic associations still succeed in providing a key for understanding Southern style as something that is Old World yet also completely au courant. Moonlight, for example, shines as brightly on Charleston, South Carolina, as it does on Paris, France, where wealthy, early nineteenth-century Southerners purchased *bronze-d'oré* chandeliers to illuminate their double parlors. While the *Magnolia grandiflora* grows elsewhere in the nation, it flourishes best in Southern soil, where some old trees have witnessed the passing of many generations beneath their branches. With deep-growing roots and fresh-scented flowers that bloom each spring, these trees are a perfect symbol for the Southerner's twin passions for past and present-day styles.

The region's undying devotion to white columns was sparked by English colonists who imported the Georgian style of architecture from their mother country. As the eighteenth and nineteenth centuries unfolded, fine Southern houses sported columns in every variation of width, height, and capital treatment—in keeping with the roster of neoclassical styles that gained favor on both sides of the Atlantic. In addition to columns, these houses boasted wide porches that were not just for show, but also for comfort. A practical necessity in the days before air-conditioning, they created a margin of man-made shade between the hot, sunny outdoors and the sheltered rooms within. Porches made it possible to keep windows and doors open without letting in rain or direct sunlight. They also serve as indicators of the varied foreign influences that shaped Southern design. While the side-porches of Charleston's single houses resemble those of the British West Indies, the narrow galleries of New Orleans' townhouses and deep porches of Louisiana plantations reveal the Creole influence—a mingling of Spanish, French, and West Indian cultures.

Spanning the front of Osborne Mackie and Morgan Delaney's townhouse, this parlor features a cornice in the French Directoire style unusual for late eighteenth-century Alexandria. Plaster busts purchased by a Virginia family enjoying the Grand Tour add more international character to the room.

A mid-nineteenth-century Venetian mirror hanging in the guest bedroom of Tom Leddy's Savannah townhouse is exquisitely detailed with blown-glass flowers in unusual shades of turquoise and olive green.

During the 1950s, it seemed you could never walk into a nice Southern house and not see chintz curtains and Chippendale-style furniture. As a result, it is hard to look at these traditional design elements with fresh eyes and see in them something that was once fashion forward. However, there was a time, a few centuries ago, when chintz curtains were considered terrifically chic and sophisticated. When the first lengths of the brightly colored, exotically patterned cloth were imported to England from India in the seventeenth century, they were highly prized—and priced—fashion fabrics. When Southerners began importing them from England, it was a sign of taste and wealth to have chintz window-hangings and bed-coverings. Many contemporary designers in the South, and beyond, are now reviving chintz, rediscovering old patterns and palettes to decorate luxuriously stylish rooms. Chintz, like good Southern style, is timeless. It is also global, weaving together the original Indian designs with their English interpretations, as well as elegant French extrapolations, including toile de Jouy.

The South's penchant for Chippendale furniture tells a similar tale. Thomas Chippendale, mid-eighteenth-century London's most successful cabinet maker, delighted patrons with ebullient furniture designs embellished with square legs or ball-and-claw feet, fluid fretwork, and florid foliation. These design details trace their inspiration to the obsession with all things Chinese that shaped the French Rococo movement and influenced England, where people were ready for a bit of decorative excess after the severity of the early Georgian style. Well-to-do Southerners, who traveled regularly to England, quickly became aware of this new style, and began bringing home furniture that, if not made in Chippendale's workshop, imitated it.

Chippendale's lasting fame grew not only out of the furniture he made, but perhaps even more so from the 1754 publication of his taste-making book, *The Gentleman and Cabinet Maker's Director*. A best-selling style publication on both sides of the Atlantic (it was reprinted in 1755, and revised and released again in 1762), the volume made it easy for expert craftsmen working in the American South to fulfill the growing demand for Chippendale-style furniture. The chairs, tables, and case pieces these Southern craftsmen

The garnishing of mantels was a high art in neoclassical American and English homes. In Charleston-based interior designer Amelia Handegan's living room, this Federal-style mantel is adorned with an unexpected array of Asian elements, including Indian white-glazed ceramics and a bronze Buddha.

This French wallpaper,
made circa 1790, reflects late
eighteenth-century Europe's
fascination with Pompeii and
Herculaneum. Installed in the
New Orleans dining room of
Sarah and Prescott Dunbar,
the wallpaper has a hand-
blocked ground with collaged
elements, including smoke
rising from incense burners.

17

This exotic Egyptian Revival pedestal reveals the French, English, and American fascination with Egypt, sparked by Napoleon's interest in the region and Lord Nelson's victory at the Battle of the Nile in 1798.

made are so refined and elegant that many furniture experts find it difficult to say whether they were constructed in England or America. Often, the only clue is the secondary wood used for drawer bottoms and backs, which in parts of the South was typically cypress—a material not found in England or the northeastern American furniture-making capitals.

Considering the worldly aesthetics of the region's eighteenth- and nineteenth-century tastes, it is puzzling that more people do not think of the South as a global and sophisticated place. Instead, the region's reputation is often dismissed as provincial and old-fashioned. The obvious culprit for this misunderstanding is the Civil War, which cut off the South from direct trade (and aesthetic) relations with England and Europe in the mid-nineteenth century. Many major capitals of Southern style were ransacked and burned, left to molder in a depressed post-war economy. Charleston, South Carolina, and Natchez, Mississippi, were among these languishing cities, where residents coping with punitive Reconstruction-era taxes could only hope to hold onto their pre-war homes and possessions. Prevented from purchasing fashionable accoutrements or building new houses, many Southerners were forced into traditionalism.

This is only half the story of the region's post-war aesthetics, however. While some Southern cities lapsed into economic torpor, others, including Savannah, New Orleans, and Atlanta, experienced even greater wealth than they had enjoyed before the war. Benefiting from the advantages of railroad and steamship transportation, which brought agricultural products, timber, and naval stores through their ports or railway hubs, these cities flourished. New residential neighborhoods sprang up with opulent homes inspired by Northeastern styles, reflecting the South's enhanced trade with the North. In the last decades of the nineteenth century, Queen Anne, Shingle style, and Richardsonian Romanesque houses became all the rage, decorated with fine furniture from New York and Philadelphia, as well as decorative items from Europe, Asia, and the Middle East.

Cities of the New South sparkled with au courant elegance from the late nineteenth century until the first decades of the twentieth, when the boll weevil ended the gilded reign of King Cotton and the Great Depression wiped out what fortunes survived. Stricken by these twin evils, for several decades the South simply could not remain a front-runner of American style. However, it *did* become a pioneer in the field of preservation, as energies were focused upon protecting the architectural vestiges of the region's former wealth and sophistication.

During the middle decades of the twentieth century, the increasing popularity of the automobile posed one of the biggest threats to the urban fabric of the South's old cities. Buildings on corner lots, often grand mansions, were torn down to be replaced by gasoline stations, and whole blocks were demolished to make space for parking lots. Venerable structures no longer in fashion fell to the wrecking ball, and others fell victim

to salvagers who sold their mantels, interior paneling, and refined moldings to the high-est bidders. In response to these threats, Susan Pringle Frost of Charleston formed the Society for the Preservation of Old Dwellings in 1920. In 1931, that city passed pioneer-ing legislation to designate America's first official historic district.

Other old Southern cities, including New Orleans, Alexandria, Virginia, and Savannah, were quick to follow suit, in hopes of increasing awareness of their historic architecture and protecting it against modern incursions. In addition, residents of these cities launched annual tours of old homes and gardens as a means to promote apprecia-tion of their historic architecture and raise funds to preserve it. For decades, ongoing events like the Natchez Pilgrimage Tours and Historic Charleston Foundation's Festival of Houses and Gardens have been offering first-hand experience of antebellum homes filled with heirlooms and old gardens redolent of boxwood and jasmine. The establish-ment of Colonial Williamsburg in 1929 as a living history museum has provided even more people with insight into the early South's architecture and decorative arts.

Southern style, when considered solely within the context of the museum, however, is all too easily defined as a relic, unrelated to what is happening in living rooms, dining rooms, and bedrooms today. One is tempted to forget that the people who purchased these objects and decorated these rooms centuries ago were the tastemakers of their times, taking aesthetic risks and enjoying the exhilarating effects. The goal of this book is to offer a broader, more vibrant point of view by looking at historic Southern decora-tive arts through the lens of the present, and at present-day styles as part of a continuum with the past. With sixteen houses selected from throughout the South, this volume offers examples ranging from historically accurate to thoroughly modern expressions of Southern aesthetics, in order to demonstrate what they all have in common.

In a section of this book entitled *Love of the New*, five houses offer examples of con-temporary Southerners—including architects Ken Tate and Tim Woods, and interior designers Nancy Braithwaite and Hal Williamson—who have successfully created new visions informed by the Old South. Whether designing a twenty-first-century Palladian villa on the Gulf Coast, mixing modern art with antiques in an Atlanta penthouse, or building a glass house with steel columns outside Savannah, these design professionals have created consciously modern residences without losing sight of the past.

Another uniting factor in Southern style is the enduring fascination with objects from afar, explored in a section entitled *Allure of the Exotic*. Dating from the earliest days of the South's history, the collection of objets d'art, rare fabrics, and fabulous furnishings from across the seas has long been a passion. Examples in this section include a town-house in Savannah ebulliently furnished in the Venetian style, a new home outside of Charleston—designed by architect Randolph Martz—with Cuban influences, and a house in New Orleans decorated with French, Indian, and Chinese accoutrements. Taken together, these houses reveal the South as a place that has always been connected both by trade and the collective imagination of its population to the entire world of style.

A third section of the book explores the *Presence of the Past*, not as something that is dead and gone, but rather alive and ever changing. Several houses in this section demonstrate the South's tradition of treasuring the past by cherishing family heirlooms

The Louis XV sofa and chairs in Debra and Jerry Shriver's New Orleans pied-à-terre reflect the strong French ties of the city. To relieve the French furniture's curvaceous lines, Hal chose contemporary Directoire-style tables in the living room and a spare, rectangular Gustavian-style table in the dining room.

and collecting antiques that complement them. Others illustrate more ingenious approaches to interpreting the region's decorative conventions. Take, for example, the wall-covering that interior designer Thomas Jayne created for his New Orleans pied-à-terre. Inspired by eighteenth- and nineteenth-century wallpapers featuring scenes of Europe and Asia, he designed a new mural based on images from a 1930s children's book about the Mississippi River. Hand-painted in China, the paper recalls the days when hand-crafted Asian export wares were de rigueur in sophisticated American and European residences.

The common thread that unites these houses and their creators is the idea of cosmopolitanism. Literally, the word means people of the cosmos—a realm where all places and all times exist simultaneously. Figuratively, the word refers to people who are urbane and sophisticated. Both definitions apply well to Southerners, who travel easily back and forth in time, and have long enjoyed global commerce in goods and ideas. And yet, the pairing of the words *Southern cosmopolitan* has occasionally raised eyebrows and even prompted the question: "Is there such a thing?" The answer is a resounding *Yes*, with proof provided in the pages of this book by the region's most worldly residents, collectors, interior designers, and architects.

With antique church lanterns hanging on weathered stucco walls, a bust of Hermes, a coral stone table from Palm Beach, and flickering candle- light from garden chandeliers, the pergola is one of the most romantic evening gathering spaces in Joane and Norman Askins' Atlanta villa.

Presence of the *Past*

In the South, the past is a living presence. It inhabits the streets and avenues, parks and covered markets of cities that retain traces of urban plans laid out by English, French, and Spanish settlers. It lies underfoot in cobblestones and overhead in roofs covered with Welsh slate—both heavy freight materials brought over as ballast by British ships. It rests on tables set with blue-and-white Chinese export ware that crossed seas in carefully packed barrels from China to England and then to America in the eighteenth and nineteenth centuries. Pieces of this well-traveled china assume place of pride on Southern tables, alongside precious heirlooms of English silver, French porcelain, and Irish crystal.

As much as Southerners enjoy telling stories about which great-great-grandparent bought what piece of tableware during a long-ago transatlantic shopping spree, they are even prouder of their Southern-made heirlooms. With so many families uprooted, possessions dispersed, and records lost during and after the Civil War, the legacy of the South's fine craftsmen was nearly lost to obscurity. The excellence of much of the region's furniture- and silver-making traditions has only recently been rediscovered and celebrated. No wonder Southern families seem to speak of their Charleston-made epergne or Natchez-made waste bowl as if it were the Holy Grail.

In the South, the past is pervasive not only on a tangible level, but also on an ethereal one, invisibly connecting every living moment with history. It is alive in the stories Southerners tell while sipping iced tea on porches or serving iced bourbon in antique julep cups in double parlors. It reveals itself through obsessions to collect furniture made in certain regions of the South or to restore houses faithfully in antebellum styles. It seduces the senses through the old-fashioned fragrance of tea olive trees, the satiny texture of polished mahogany, the taste of China tea, the sound of old church bells, and the sight of softly faded silk velvet. In the South, the past is a spirit that infuses everything, reminding us to live our lives as daringly, stylishly, and sensually as our ancestors did. Far from being dead and gone, the past is alive and well, forming a bridge to the future that invites Southerners to live for the day, because tomorrow, they might just be remembered.

Creole Collage

In collaboration with de Gournay, Thomas Jayne designed this scenic wallpaper dominated by the mud-gold swells and currents of the Mississippi River. The simple ceilings and moldings, in keeping with traditional Creole style, provide a restrained setting for the high-impact mural paper.

Thomas Jayne, a New York–based interior designer with California roots, has long been interested in Southern decorative arts, in part, he explains, because the region is the most history obsessed in the nation. During his training in American architecture and decorative arts at Winterthur Museum in Delaware, Thomas honed his fascination with eighteenth- and nineteenth-century decorative arts into a refined expertise. Today, he uses this knowledge to create historically accurate interiors for preservation-minded clients, as well as projects exploring the spirit of creative anachronism. The New Orleans pied-à-terre Thomas created recently as a weekend escape for himself and partner Rick Ellis falls quite wonderfully into the latter category.

The small apartment is located on the second floor of a Creole townhouse. Built in 1836, the brick building boasts a *garçonnière* possibly dating from the eighteenth century. In keeping with the traditional design of such dwellings, the narrow building has a simply adorned facade, with wrought-iron balconies on the upper floors and an arched entrance leading from the street into a small courtyard. Within this sheltered space, stairs ascend to narrow porches, called galleries by the Creoles, which open into the rooms of the townhouse. Once a single-family residence, the Creole dwelling now has several tenants who live in the main building as well as a narrow ell behind.

Ethnically, the word *Creole* refers to people born in the New World, whether in the Caribbean or America, who trace their lineage to French or Spanish ancestors. Stylistically, the term evokes visions of spare yet elegantly decorated rooms filled with a mix of French and American-made furniture and decorative arts. "In the South, there is a wonderful synthesis of cultures," says Thomas. "In New Orleans, you have Spanish underpinnings of a French culture. And, just as importantly, you have the culture of the city's English, Irish, and Italian populations, which are often discounted. This mixture of influences is what made the city's old interiors so cosmopolitan."

While Thomas prefers keeping the mural room's gondola chairs flush against the walls, Rick likes to pull these French armchairs to the table, creating a more relaxed air. The room's mustard-colored moldings repeat one of the many shades of gold found in the wallpaper.

29

While the decor of Thomas and Rick's apartment reflects most of these influences, the interior is anything but a slavish imitation of Old French Quarter style. Working with renowned New Orleans architect, the late Frank Masson, Thomas merged the spirit and palette of Creole style with a luxurious global design aesthetic. This marriage is best illustrated by the apartment's large entertaining room—an architecturally restrained space that forms a perfect backdrop for dazzling scenic wallpaper designed by Thomas. The tradition of scenic wallpaper, called *papiers peints panoramiques* in France, began in the late eighteenth century, when French artisans vied with each other to create the most elaborate designs. All the rage in period French, English, and Anglo-Colonial houses, its popularity has endured into the present in the South, spurring Thomas to comment, "There may be more scenic wallpaper per capita in the South than anywhere else in the nation."

The designer decided to perpetuate that tradition in his New Orleans pied-à-terre. Rather than purchase one of the reproduction patterns available, Thomas preferred to create his own. "I was concerned that many of the subjects of historical panoramic wallpaper might seem out of place or pretentious in this small townhouse," he said. So instead of covering his walls with *Monuments of Paris* or *Scenes of North America*, Thomas opted for a homegrown theme inspired by a children's book given to him by his grandparents called *The Story of the Mississippi*, written by Marshall McClintock and illustrated by Works Progress Administration artist C. H. DeWitt.

FAR LEFT Reproduction woodblock wallpaper, a nineteenth-century Jacquard coverlet, and the Persian carpet create a dynamic mix of color, texture, and pattern to the bedroom. American gondola chairs flank the entrance and Audubon's *Californian Vulture* hangs above the bed.

LEFT A French clock, circa 1830, with extravagant ormolu garniture, reveals the contrast between lavish continental European fashion and the simpler styles afforded by French Creole expatriates of the same period.

In classic Creole style, narrow wood galleries overlooking the courtyard connect the rooms of this French Quarter townhouse with those of the *garçonnière*, or outbuilding, behind. French doors bring light and air into the apartments, while board-and-batten shutters offer protection from the sun and intruders.

Thomas created the paper in collaboration with de Gournay, an English firm, which, in keeping with the tradition of the British East India Company, provides custom wallpapers, fabrics, and porcelain hand-painted in China for Western clients. The scenes of Thomas's one-of-a-kind paper depict a Creole plantation house, the Battle of New Orleans, workers unloading cotton from a steamboat, and a country picnic—all linked by the mud-gold swells of the Mississippi River. "Most traditional mural papers employ a single horizon line that lends them a measured, formal air," say Thomas, who opted instead for a more imploded sense of space. In this design, the river's dizzying swirls and eddies create the impression that one is standing not in a room, but on a raft in the center of the Mississippi's currents.

In order to allow the wallpaper to shine without competition, the rest of the room's decor adheres to a restrained Creole aesthetic. The room's woodwork is painted with a popular Creole color scheme of mustard gold and blue. Canton matting from China, a floor covering historically employed by Southerners in the summertime, covers the floor. Plain linen curtains filter the sun that enters the room through the narrow French windows opening to the balcony. Originally Thomas considered having no curtains, but Rick insisted upon them, and Thomas concurred. "Curtains are such a Southern thing," he notes. "A room without curtains in the South would be very eccentric."

In keeping with Creole tradition, most of the room's furniture, including a simple bench and several gondola chairs, are pushed against the outer walls of the room. In the center, a simple covering of red linen with a grosgrain ribbon edge drapes a large, round table. "The Creole style is about using simple materials elegantly," says Thomas, explaining that this was a practical necessity in the eighteenth- and early nineteenth-centuries, when elaboration was costly.

Similar restraint is evidenced in the *salon rose*, as Thomas and Rick refer to a small sitting room. In yet another nod to Creole style, most of the rooms are multipurpose, making it hard to use typical nomenclature. Serving both as a guest room and a place to enjoy drinks with friends, this room combines the masculine forms of a French Empire daybed with a feminine, rose-colored toile. Although the tall woodblock prints of clowns hanging above the daybed are from Germany, they might just as easily be portraits of New Orleanians dressed for Mardi Gras. Suggestive of the city's more serious side, an English Midlands pottery figure depicting Fortitude as a woman holding a broken column offers a perfect symbol for post-Katrina New Orleans.

In the master bedroom, Thomas chose a more personal symbol in the large Audubon print that hangs over the bed depicting what Audubon termed a "California Vulture." "I've always been drawn to that image because I love condors and I'm from California," he explains. "It's not highly valued among Audubon's bird prints because it's so hideous, but I think it's wonderful." The designer also chose the print because he felt it could hold its own when hung against floral wallpaper based on a two-hundred-year-old pattern that he revived in collaboration with Colonial Williamsburg historian Margaret Pritchard and Adelphi Paper Hangings.

A mahogany bed, a reproduction of an early nineteenth-century Creole piece owned by friend and antiques dealer Peter Patout, dominates the small room, which has little space for much else. A nineteenth-century Jacquard coverlet adorns the bed, adding yet another note of pattern to the room. "There are times when pattern can actually make a room appear larger than it is," Thomas notes. The bedroom's single, large window opens onto the jasmine-scented courtyard where the sounds of steamship whistles and horse-drawn carriages echo, competing with muffled music from nearby Bourbon Street and honking automobiles. Here, as elsewhere in this pied-à-terre, the past and the present, the European and the American, the urban and the tropical all combine to create a perfect Creole collage.

A River Runs Through It

Built in 1835 by cotton planter William Harris, this Natchez house was significantly remodeled in 1855 by Nathaniel Carpenter, who is believed to have added the neoclassical porch.

New Orleans-based interior decorator Hal Williamson and physician Dale LeBlanc visited Natchez, Mississippi, not long after Hurricane Katrina ravaged their Garden District neighborhood. Well north and west of the hurricane's path, Natchez offered a calm respite from the post-storm stress of New Orleans. Hal recalls a day when he and Dale leisurely explored the town's urban homes and outlying plantations. "It was really like a dream, seeing the old homes, the moss-draped trees, and the panoramic views from the bluffs," he says. As the light began to fade, Dale exclaimed, "It's as if God reached his hands into the heavens, grabbed a handful of stars, tossed them to the ground, and they became the beautiful homes of Natchez."

While the actual story of Natchez's development as a major river port is not quite so pretty, it's fascinating nonetheless. Originally a settlement of Natchez Indians, the four-hundred-foot-high bluff above the Mississippi River commands a strategic point between the upper Mississippi and the lower reaches that lead to the river's mouth. Every ambitious European explorer who encountered the towering river bluff recognized its economic and political importance. French explorer René-Robert Cavelier, Sieur de La Salle, noted its potential for controlling Mississippi River traffic in 1682. Jean-Baptiste Le Moyne, Sieur de Bienville, claimed it for Louis XV in 1716. The conquering English established a small town at the foot of the bluffs called Natchez Landing in 1763. Spanish invaders reclaimed Natchez from the English in 1779. And finally, the Americans, who by this time possessed the far side of the river, took Natchez from Spain in 1798.

Then in 1811 the first steamboat to paddle down the Mississippi and dock at Natchez-Under-The-Hill set in motion a chain of events that led to Natchez boasting more millionaires in 1830 than any other American city, save New York. Agricultural products from up the Mississippi—especially cotton, which was grown with great success in and around Natchez—passed through the river port, enriching it until the Union army invaded the town in 1863, ending the reign of King Cotton.

The built environment of the small city reflects this history, beginning with the urban design of the town—a relic of the Spaniards who laid it out. The houses that line the town's streets, though constructed for the most part by wealthy Americans, are furnished mostly with French and English antiques. In the prosperous antebellum era, stately in-town mansions and monumental plantation houses in a variety of classical styles sprang up along the river. Because its popularity coincided with the peak of the town's wealth, the boldly romantic Greek Revival style is most closely associated with Natchez. However, houses built in the 1810s and 1820s reveal the more delicate elegance of the Federal style, and mid-nineteenth-century dwellings boast sophisticated Italianate forms including paired columns and double- or triple-arched windows.

When Hal and Dale decided they had to have one of the stars God tossed down to make Natchez, they opted for an Italianate villa with a Greek Revival interior. The house is known as the William Harris House, named for its first occupant and builder, an early planter and the father of Confederate General Nathaniel Harris. While building this relatively restrained townhouse, Harris was also supervising the construction of Ravenna, a plantation house considered to be one of the first grand Greek Revival homes in Natchez. With its double porch and slender Doric columns, his house in town, circa 1835 (and remodeled in 1855 by its second owner, Nathaniel Carpenter), was far more conservative in style than the bold country house.

In keeping with the typical double-house plan popular in the South, a wide center hall runs through the dwelling, connecting four rooms on the ground floor. Hal decorated these with English, American, and French antiques that celebrate three of the five cultures associated with Natchez. French objects dominate the center hall, where a Louis XVI chair sits next to an Empire commode of glowing walnut with bright ormolu garniture. Above the commode hangs an exquisite trumeau mirror with a painted scene from the popular eighteenth-century French novel *Paul et Virginie*. An Oushak carpet with a subdued pattern and softly faded shades of gray and amber interjects a contemporary, relaxed mood into the space.

To one side of the center hall, a pair of fluted Ionic columns frames the entrance to the drawing room, making it quite clear to guests that they are invited in. "I always thought New Orleans was one of the friendliest cities in the world," says Hal. "But Natchez, with its gorgeous homes and the charm of its citizens, takes hospitality to another whole level." The only asymmetrical room in the house, the polygonal drawing room has a long wall on one side that Hal thought the perfect place for a pianoforte, a musical instrument frequently used to accompany dancing and singing during nineteenth-century entertainments. After purchasing a pianoforte at auction from a Mississippi estate, Hal discovered that it was numbered, dated, and signed by the maker who also produced a pianoforte for Thomas Jefferson.

Another of Hal's great finds for the room is a Scottish chaise he discovered in a Natchez antiques shop. Being of Scotch heritage, Hal was interested in the history of this piece. As a New Orleanian, he was intrigued to discover fleurs-de-lis—a symbol of the city—among the metal inlay on the piece. And as a designer, he loved the rare old

Hal Williamson chose a carpet runner for the center hall stairs that reproduces an oak leaf pattern from the Biltmore Estate and is fabricated by English company Wilton Mills. "The oak motif reminded me of all the ancient oaks that shade the streets and plantations of Natchez," he says.

rosewood from which it was made. A Pierre Frey fabric with aqua-and-white stripes covers the piece, offering crisp contrast to its curving lines. Across the room, an early nineteenth-century American classical sofa with scroll arms and muted turquoise silk upholstery complements the Scottish piece.

Throughout the ground floor, the same spectrum of blues and greens mingled with touches of lavender and black prevails. Both Hal and Dale grew up near water—Dale in Pass Christian, Mississippi, and Hal, a native Georgian, on visits to his family lakeside home in Winter Park, Florida, and later, as a resident of Palm Beach. "We are drawn to watery colors, and here we are right on the Mississippi," says Hal. "So I went with aqua, turquoise, sea green, the color of sea grass, and walls the color of wet sand or stone." The *Monuments of Paris* scenic wallpaper Hal and Dale chose for the dining room pulls all these tones together, adding touches of beige, antique red, and rich browns.

LEFT A pair of fluted columns creates a ceremonial entrance to the primary entertaining room, a polygonal parlor furnished with an American classical sofa, English Regency chairs, and an English secretary, circa 1830, decorated with an eagle motif.

RIGHT Hal upholstered an early nineteenth-century classical sofa from Philadelphia in patterned silk from Mulberry to complement the parlor's palette. While most of the room's furniture is American, the secretary bookcase behind the sofa is an early nineteenth-century English piece.

OVERLEAF The blue waters of the Seine, a boundary of verdant trees, and elegant nineteenth-century buildings, as depicted in this reproduction of Joseph Darfour's 1814 *Monuments of Paris* wallpaper, remind Hal and Dale of the Mississippi River and the glory of the Cotton Kingdom of Natchez.

Designed in France in 1814 by Joseph Darfour, the wallpaper depicts scenes of Parisian life against a backdrop of the city's most opulent palaces and monuments, many of which no longer exist. Laboriously manufactured with thousands of hand-carved woodblocks and hundreds of colors, the wallpaper was used by Napoleon at Fontainebleau and George Washington at Mount Vernon. A faithful reproduction, produced in a limited edition, was created in 1977 by Twigs, in association with the Metropolitan Museum of Art.

"We chose it because we like scenic wallpaper, and we love Paris, but most of all because a river runs through it, and in Natchez, you are always aware that a river runs by the town and is the main reason for its existence," says Dale. Hal adds, "If you look closely, you see scenes of men riding on horseback, which call to mind the early years in Natchez, when horse racing was popular. There are elegant ladies strolling along the river, children playing, people swimming, flatboats floating, which are all things you would have seen in Natchez in the nineteenth century."

For dinner parties, Hal and Dale love to set the table with a brilliant assembly of porcelain, silver, and crystal. Years of collecting sprees stock their china cabinet full of Old Paris porcelain, fine silver serving pieces, and antique crystal—both delicate stemware and weighty cut glass. One of Hal's favorite discoveries was a set of Old Paris porcelain, including a large tureen and platter, with a violet rim. Having never before encountered the porcelain in that shade, he snapped them up, as well as a set of oyster plates with turquoise and gold decoration. Together the two patterns create a vibrant table setting, made even more brilliant with the addition of bright aqua crystal cruets from France.

LEFT Images of well-to-do Parisians riding and frolicking on the banks of the Seine are not at all unlike scenes that unfolded along the Mississippi at the height of the cotton boom. Natchez-made silver, including an exquisite footed waste bowl, stand on an English sideboard.

RIGHT With four guestrooms, Hal and Dale's house is always ready for a house party. This suite, which includes a large soaking tub original to the house, combines many of Hal's signature contrasting elements, in this case a black *tôle* bed against a soft blue wall, and a painted country table offsetting a more formal Louis Philippe secretary.

Among the most cherished objects in this opulent trove of tableware is a small selection of Natchez-made silver. "Only American towns of great wealth could support their own silversmiths, and Natchez was one of them," says Hal, who is excited to possess a waste bowl. Designed to hold discarded lemon slices and tea leaves as part of a tea service, the bowl is made by Emile Profilet, one of the city's best-known silversmiths. Hal also found a ladle made by Samuel Cockrell, another important Natchez silversmith, and several smaller silver pieces. "These old pieces give us a glimpse of history," says Dale. "When we use them, we connect directly with Natchez's past."

Objets de Luxe

HOUSE OF MORGAN D. DELANEY AND OSBORNE PHINIZY MACKIE
ALEXANDRIA, VIRGINIA

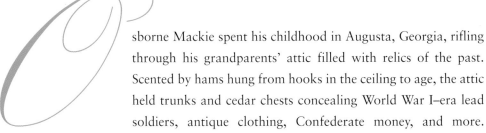

While most of the surrounding Old Town, Alexandria, townhouses are two or three bays wide, the late eighteenth-century merchant's house (second building on right) where Morgan Delaney and Osborne Mackie live has four bays. The ground floor has been used as a commercial space, with a residence above, since its construction in 1797 for French merchant Bernard de Ghequiere.

Osborne Mackie spent his childhood in Augusta, Georgia, rifling through his grandparents' attic filled with relics of the past. Scented by hams hung from hooks in the ceiling to age, the attic held trunks and cedar chests concealing World War I–era lead soldiers, antique clothing, Confederate money, and more. Before he knew it, young Osborne became an impassioned collector, starting with stinkbugs and shark's teeth, graduating to coins and stamps, and finally settling upon seashells, which he labeled and organized into his own museum.

Morgan Delaney's early fascination with history stemmed from the experience of growing up in an 1820s townhouse in Alexandria, Virginia, that was filled with antiques. His uncle Paul Delaney played a major role in establishing Old Town, Alexandria, as America's third historic district in 1946 (following the pioneering designations of Charleston and New Orleans' Vieux Carré). So it is not surprising that Morgan became interested both in collecting antiques and preserving and restoring old houses. He has owned three in Alexandria, beginning with a Victorian row house, followed by a Federal townhouse built in the early 1800s, and finally, the late eighteenth-century townhouse he shares with Osborne. The two collectors have decorated the townhouse with inherited and acquired objects including fine furniture made in the American South and late eighteenth- and early nineteenth-century decorative objects and fine art from America and Europe.

Osborne's interest in collecting furniture and decorative objects began when his family relocated to Europe when he was nine. "We spent summers in Scotland, where we visited relatives living in an ancient castle and saw many country houses filled with wonderful things," Osborne recalls. After attending boarding school at Glenalmond in Perth, Osborne reluctantly returned to America. "I can't express how much I missed the romance that had defined my life up to that point." When he entered graduate school in architectural history at the University of Virginia, he rented a little log cabin outside Charlottesville and began to furnish it. "I had to have a collection for my house," he says.

LEFT A family portrait painted in
Paris in 1809 and passed down to
Osborne hangs in the grand drawing
room, surrounded by late eighteenth-
century sepia stipple engravings of
paintings by Angelika Kaufmann.

ABOVE A small eighteenth-century
Paris porcelain covered bullion bowl
is decorated with a pattern of undulat-
ing lines referred to as *Arabesque*. A
similar pattern is found in the drawing
room's cornice molding, also French in
style and designed in the same period.

LEFT Ferdinand Phinizy, depicted in this watercolor-on-ivory portrait miniature, is Osborne's great-great-great-great-grandfather. He emigrated from Parma, Italy, to Georgia in the 1780s, where he made a fortune in cotton. This portrait, painted circa 1795, depicts him with a snowy white cravat and pompadour befitting a wealthy European expatriate.

RIGHT A harp stool made by Georgetown cabinetmaker William King, circa 1815, has shed its old upholstery, revealing a tangle of horsehair. Black jasperware medallions, a Derby biscuit figure inspired by a mythological painting by Angelika Kaufmann, and a Wedgwood and Bentley basalt urn are among the exquisite mantel garniture.

A period of enthusiastic buying sprees at estate sales ensued, during which Osborne collected without a strong central focus. When he became director of Tudor Place, a neo-classical house museum in Georgetown built by one of Martha Washington's grand-daughters, he learned about American collections and their management, and became concerned that his own collection lacked discipline. "I was talking to a British friend, and I said, maybe I should collect porcelain," Osborne recounts. "My friend answered lofti-ly that 'The best porcelain are *objets de luxe*, and you will *never* be able to afford them.'" Spurred on by this challenge, Osborne replied, "Ha! I'm going to collect porcelain." And so he has.

At first, Osborne revisited his childhood love of shells, collecting English and European porcelain with shell motifs. Among his first purchases was an early nineteenth-century Worcester tea service with transfer-printed shells. The collector's interest in porce-lains has since expanded to include eighteenth-century figures, particularly mythological

Four family portraits, including the upper-right portrait of Dr. Isaac Hill by George Romney, surround the large library bookcase made by Alexandria cabinetmaker John Muir. A Baltimore classical sofa with saber legs and sapphirine upholstery is flanked by two Baltimore fancy chairs.

and allegorical subjects. Mars and Venus, Jupiter and Juno, the Seasons and the Senses have all found their places on tabletops and mantels in the collectors' townhouse. Morgan and Osborne also share a fascination with Swiss artist Angelika Kaufmann, who achieved great success as a portraitist and history painter in eighteenth-century Europe. A pair of Derby biscuit groups based on her depictions of Greek myths stand on the drawing room mantel and sepia stipple engravings derived from her work hang nearby.

Delicately detailed and brightly colored figures made by Derby, Chelsea, and Bow— the three leading English makers of porcelain in the eighteenth century—decorate the dining room's table and sideboards. Four figures made by Chelsea, circa 1755, to represent The Continents stand on a classical marble-topped sideboard. "*America* is a woman in a feather headdress, holding a bow and arrow, standing next to a very odd, rather friendly looking alligator," explains Osborne. Two rustic maidens, a tipsy swain, and a shivering old man from the Bow factory represent the seasons, and a lithesome Diana made by Derby, circa 1760, is typical of the classical figures popular at that time.

While these small decorative objects add charm and interest to the surroundings, it is the large pieces, including Osborne's oversize family portraits and Morgan's eighteenth-century library bookcase, that create the greatest impact. These pieces are so large that their owners had difficulty finding a house spacious enough to accommodate them. "We discovered that the portraits wouldn't fit up the stairs of my previous townhouse," says Morgan. This dilemma led to the purchase of a 1797 townhouse built by French émigré Bernard de Ghequiere. Morgan surmises that Ghequiere, accustomed to the grander proportions of aristocratic European townhouses, commissioned his building to have four bays, rather than the two or three bays common to most Old Town dwellings in Alexandria.

On its second floor, the townhouse boasts an unusually commodious drawing room measuring 20 by 30 feet with a 13-foot ceiling. While the rooms of neighboring houses from the same period are strictly English in style, this room is crowned by a plaster cornice with an *Arabesque* pattern popular in France during the Directoire period. "Ghequiere probably brought the molds over with him from France when he came in 1792," says Osborne.

The room proves the perfect setting for the largest of Osborne's family portraits, a composition with three figures: Boston ancestress Hannah Skinner Church, her daughter, and her English daughter-in-law. Painted in 1809 by French artist Jacques Antoine Vallin, this and two other family portraits commissioned at the same time may be the only full-length portraits of Americans painted in Empire France, according to Osborne. This painting depicts an emotionally charged moment in the lives of the three women, occasioned by a letter of betrayal, which one of the women has just finished reading.

Although the scale is decidedly smaller, the portrait miniature on ivory of Osborne's ancestor Ferdinand Phinizy is equally compelling. Phinizy moved in the eighteenth century from Parma, Italy, to Augusta, Georgia, where he made a fortune in cotton. With sensual Italian features and a powdered pompadour every bit as white and frothy as his lace neckerchief, Phinizy is a worthy courtier of King Cotton.

LEFT Following the success of Meissen and Sèvres, English porcelain makers came into their own in the 1760s. Osborne collected four figures made by the Chelsea factory, circa 1765, depicting the continents, including this turbaned lady on a camel representing Asia.

RIGHT The unusual width of Ghequire's house creates a dining room spacious enough to accommodate two large sideboards, including the Federal Norfolk sideboard on the far wall, and the Charles X pier mirror above it. Used commonly in dining rooms, such mirrors amplify the candlelight and glittering array of silver, glass, and fine porcelain arrayed on the dining table.

A massive library bookcase Morgan inherited, which once belonged to George Washington's physician Dr. Elisha Cullen Dick, was another heirloom that demanded space. Made by Alexandria cabinetmaker John Muir, the piece has magnificent cabriole feet that had been removed in order to fit it into Morgan's previous residence. Morgan also needed a large drawing room for his two neoclassical Virginia sofas, circa 1800, and a Grecian sofa from Baltimore with saber legs and volute arms. These are arranged in seating areas on either side of a rare Baltimore marble-topped center table, circa 1820.

Osborne and Morgan entertain frequently, enjoying candlelit dinners in the dining room, which has only one electric lamp but a plenitude of wall sconces and candelabra and an eighteenth-century cut-glass chandelier. Such gatherings begin and end with interludes of conversation surrounded by the gleaming wood and lustrous silk of the drawing room. The small sitting room at the back of the house, furnished with fine Virginia antiques, is a favorite haunt for quiet evenings at home. But even for moments of solitude, Morgan and Osborne often gravitate toward the grand drawing room and its glittering array of *objets de luxe*. "It's the most wonderful place for musing," says Osborne.

Romancing the Past

HOUSE OF JOANE AND NORMAN ASKINS: ATLANTA, GEORGIA

It took only thirteen months to build the Italianate villa where Joane and Norman Askins live in Atlanta, Georgia, but if you ask them, they will tell you (with a twinkle of the eye) that it actually took centuries. "It's an old Italian farmhouse that has been lived in and added onto for generations," says Norman, one of Atlanta's leading architects and a lover of old houses. To prove his point, Norman points to a large casement window in the living room with leaded panes of glass that looks much older than most of the house's other windows. Of course, the glass is restoration glass, and the story, pure fiction. But the house's aura of romance is one-hundred-percent genuine, thanks to the passion for and knowledge about Old World style that Joane and Norman share.

"I've loved old houses all my life," declares Norman, who grew up visiting venerable homes and antiques shops in Alabama, studied architectural history at the University of Virginia, attended the prestigious Attingham Trust summer study program in England, and toured Europe extensively. As one of the South's finest architects working in traditional styles, he started out designing Colonial Revival houses during the Williamsburg craze of the 1960s, moving on to Georgian-, French-, Italianate-, and, most recently, English Arts and Crafts–style dwellings. Despite his interest in a wide range of historic styles, Norman's own personal preference is for Italian architecture.

"It's kind of the mother lode," he explains. "Italy is where everything came from—and the elements of Italian houses make perfect sense in the American South: big overhangs, stucco walls, tile floors, high ceilings, loggias, porches, pergolas." Norman proves this point with the upscale Italian farmhouse he designed as his residence. The pale stucco facade of the house, ornamented with a pedimented front doorway and shaded by an overhanging tiled roof, promises shelter from the Georgia heat. Within, plaster walls and tile floors create cool surfaces for fingers and feet, and casement windows frame garden

views that refresh the eyes. High ceilings draw hot air up on summer days, while carved stone mantels frame large fireplaces that provide winter warmth. While Norman and Joane do use modern heat and air-conditioning when necessary, they find that these classic Italian features often help them do without.

Also taking cues from Italian farmhouses, the architectural detailing of the interior spaces is pure and simple. "No baseboards (except in the upstairs rooms), very few cornices, no trim around the windows," notes Norman. "Everything is simple, simple, simple. It's all about proportion and scale." And this is a good thing, considering that the couple's approach to interior design is lushly layered. While Norman enjoys collaborating on the interior decoration of the houses he designs, Joane is the official interior decorator of their own home. Her interest in interior design began when she was a young girl in Texas, culminating in a trip to Europe in her twenties. "Everything I thought was wonderful was right before my eyes," she recalls. In particular, Joane fell in love with French, Spanish, and Italian decor. "I love the patina you see in those interiors, and the fact that these people didn't just go out and buy everything new," she says. "They inherited their possessions, and if they look old and worn, they liked them even more."

LEFT An elaborately carved, seventeenth-century Italian cabinet stands in the corner of the dining room next to a window embellished with a custom wrought-iron rod and valence of antique velvet vestments. In Old World style, a Persian gallery rug covers a long table decorated with nineteenth-century majolica urns.

ABOVE The kitchen's Italian chandelier has both real candles and electric lights, allowing for just the right amount of illumination and romance. English and American pottery, much of it Southern, is arranged upon ledges beneath the room's barrel-vaulted ceiling.

This loggia-like space has large windows on three sides, as well as French doors that open to a paved terrace. In addition to offering an ideal place to enjoy the garden in bloom from spring through autumn, the room's heated floor makes it a comfortable sunroom in winter.

Although Joane and Norman actually did go out and buy many of the furnishings for their house—admittedly over several decades—it doesn't look that way. Much of the furniture and decorative objects are Italian, dating from the seventeenth and eighteenth centuries. Joane combined these expertly with objects from other European countries and well-chosen contemporary pieces. In the living room, for example, an eighteenth-century Flemish verdure tapestry hangs above a sofa newly upholstered with slate gray velvet. Another tapestry (this time a reproduction) drapes a round table covered with Russian icons, which Joane loves, she says, for "their beauty and patina, and the stories they tell." More icons decorate a huge stone fireplace carved in France in reproduction of a mantel at Crane Cottage, a late nineteenth-century Italianate villa on Jeckyl Island, Georgia. The room's eclectic contents also include a Chinese coramandel screen, a Hudson River School landscape, and an early sixteenth-century wooden sculpture of a Madonna and Child so old that the faces have rubbed off.

Sepia-toned velvet curtains hang from heavy iron curtain poles above the living room's leaded-glass casement windows, which were inspired by an old country villa in Vicenza. "This is the seventeenth-century part of the farmhouse," says Norman, explaining his home's fictional history. "The rest was added in the eighteenth century." A ceiling crisscrossed with weathered beams reinforces the room's appearance of age, as does an antique Italian chandelier of iron that casts a soft light. "I am proud to say that there is not a single canned light in this house," says Norman.

In contrast to the sensuous decor of the living room, the dining room has a more severe air, which, Norman explains, is more in keeping with traditional Italian country style. The white plaster ceiling has simple, geometric moldings and the floor of antique terra-cotta tile is unadorned by carpets. Only two paintings—albeit fine ones—hang on walls covered with hand-troweled and tinted plaster. Valences made from ancient velvet altar decorations hang from hand-forged curtain rods of twisted iron. An antique priest's vestment runs down the center of the long dining room table, layered on top of an antique gallery rug. Completing the room's simple decor is a seventeenth-century Italian cabinet and twelve eighteenth-century Tuscan walnut chairs.

Intimate dinners are often served in the kitchen, which Norman designed with a barrel-vaulted roof inspired by the kitchens of old French and Italian country houses. The kitchen has no refrigerator or modern cabinetry; these up-to-date amenities are hidden in an adjacent butler's pantry. It does have a fireplace that the Askins light daily in fall and winter. An antique French farmhouse table stands next to the hearth, surrounded by mismatched chairs that provide comfortable, informal seating.

A pair of glazed doors leads from the kitchen to a room with large windows and braided columns that frame views of the garden behind the house. This terraced landscape was inspired by the gardens of La Foce, a villa on the border of Umbria and Tuscany that is one of the Askins' favorite places. The airiest room in the house, this loggia-like space is decorated with an eighteenth-century Italian credenza and a French daybed, both painted a powdery pale blue. Blue-and-white Chinese export ware and silver velvet upholstery reinforce the cool color scheme, while a zebra skin rug adds a touch of whimsy. "We never want the house to look too serious," says Norman.

LEFT Padded walls, curtains of rose-colored damask, and the nineteenth-century daybed's antique red-and-white toile upholstery create a warm and softly feathered nest in Joane's office.

RIGHT A heavily carved antique European door opens into a fanciful powder room, where an eighteenth-century Italian fountain serves as a lavatory. Antique French lace hangs gauzily over the windows and shell mirrors echo the baroque forms of the lavatory.

This statement is made quite clear from the start, thanks to a lifesize portrait of Norman and Joane in Renaissance-style costumes that fills an arched niche in the entry hall. Norman holds the house plans in his hands while Joane appears to curtsey to guests as they pass the fresco-like portraits created by artist Jill Biskin, who once painted sets for New York City's Metropolitan Opera. Like many an Italian opera, the story told by Norman and Joane's house is a romance. And while the two principal players *are* in love, the story is also a romance in the earlier definition of the word: a story about the days of old. Romancing the past and bringing it into the present, these two design professionals reveal the South's enduring love affair with Old World style.

ABOVE Viewed from the master bedroom's balcony, the garden reveals its perfect symmetry and graceful terracing. While the statuary and large terra-cotta urns came from France, the fountain's quatrefoil basin was salvaged from a Mediterranean Revival building in Florida.

RIGHT An antique cast-stone urn from France, decorated with rams' heads and scenes from classical mythology, serves as a fountain in the center of the terraced garden. Classical statues from France stand on either side of steps leading to the garden's upper terrace.

High Style

HOUSE OF SARAH AND PRESCOTT DUNBAR: NEW ORLEANS, LOUISIANA

Fashioned in the Meissen porcelain workshop during the Joachim Johann Kändler period (1730–1775), this large, fanciful figure of an Orientalist potentate astride a rhinoceros garnishes a mantel in the home of Sarah and Prescott Dunbar.

Prescott Dunbar began his lifelong fascination with objects and their history as a teenager, tagging along with family friend Felix Kuntz, whose collection of colonial American furniture and paintings now fills two rooms at the New Orleans Museum of Art. Young Prescott and his father, who lived in Baton Rouge, would accompany Mr. Kuntz on collecting forays to St. Francisville and Opelousas in Louisiana, and Natchez, Mississippi. Expeditions turned up not only furniture, but also rare first editions, documents, and historic maps, many dealing with the Louisiana Purchase Territory, which now form a seminal portion of Tulane University's rare book collection.

Not surprisingly, Prescott concentrated in history during his undergraduate years at the University of the South, in Tennessee, and later as a Ford Fellow at Harvard University, where he studied medieval history. While in Boston, he met a young woman named Sarah Blodgett who also came from a family of art and furniture collectors and had recently completed a bachelor of fine arts degree at Syracuse University. The two soon became engaged, beginning a lifetime of passionate collecting. The first object they bought was a Philadelphia Chippendale mahogany highboy, circa 1765, with exquisitely delicate fretwork and scrolls.

The rarefied collection Sarah and Prescott have since amassed embodies the term "high style," which connotes the ultimate, most ebullient, even exaggerated expression of a form or period of design. It is to pieces of this quality that the Dunbars are continually drawn in their constant search for new objects that stimulate their evolving tastes. Whether purchasing rare furniture, such as an elaborately carved tester bed, or creating entire period rooms, like their Chinese Room with hand-painted wallpaper and fanciful rococo furnishings, they drift toward the most lavish *objets de luxe*.

As a family of collectors, the Dunbars and their sons Hayden, a contemporary art dealer, and Lander, an antiquarian, are catholic in their tastes. Their Greek Revival home in the Garden District of New Orleans is evocative of the great country houses of

A marble-topped tea table in the Dunbars' blue parlor is one of the many rare pieces in their collection. Unlike most American Chippendale-style tea tables, this piece by Newport cabinetmakers Townsend and Goddard has articulated ball-and-claw feet, so called because of the open spaces between the ball and claw.

England, where extended families, dogs, guests, and servants all occupy gracious rooms filled with portraits, fine furniture, and disparate objects acquired by their forebears. While caring for family heirlooms, the Dunbars also perpetuate familial fascinations—including Prescott's interest in colonial American furniture and Sarah's memory of her grandmother's Chinese writing room in Grand Rapids, Michigan.

During their travels, the Dunbars encountered Chinese rooms in Sturbridge Village, Massachusetts; Colonial Williamsburg, Virginia; and Claydon Park and Nostell Priory in England, inspiring them to create one of their own. "The sheer whimsy of the painted decoration, combined with the highly carved gilt ornamentation, makes the room simultaneously breathtaking and endearing to me," says Sarah. Used by the family (and their Pekingneses, Theseus, Pandora, and Hercules) as an informal sitting room, the Dunbars' Chinese room is lined with hand-painted wallpaper, custom-made by Gracey and Company. Based on the decorations of an eighteenth-century room in a Massachusetts home, the paper is painted with a riot of birds, butterflies, trees, and flowers. The wallpaper and matching fabric draperies create a cerulean backdrop for the curvaceous forms of English and French rococo decorative objects, including a carved and gilt-gessoed "Tree of Life" table made by English cabinetmaker and Chippendale contemporary Thomas Johnson. The gleaming base of the table depicts Aesop's fable of the shepherd catching the wolf in sheep's clothing—a unique subject for such a piece, suggesting that it may have been a special commission.

The hand-painted wallpaper in
the Dunbars' Chinese room is
copied after panels of Chinese
export wallpaper that decorated
a room in an eighteenth-century
house in Massachusetts.
Figures on the gilded "Tree of
Life" table depict a scene from
one of Aesop's fables.

A pair of delightful Louis XV fancy paintings of Chinese figures is surrounded in unfettered rococo style with gilded garlands, scallop shells, dragons, and foliation.

Also enhancing the room is an ornately carved Chinese Chippendale mantel and over-mantel of Scotch pine. Originally gilded, the piece has gradually returned to a natural wood-grained patina. While the "Tree of Life" table has a fulsome quality in its carving, the Chippendale mantel demonstrates a more delicate, attenuated style that complements the wallpaper's graceful bamboo stalks and peony stems. The mantel is flanked by a pair of Louis XV panels with fanciful Chinese scenes encased by gilt-wood rococo frames decorated with dragons, scallop shells, and waterfall details. "These are the most exuberant, fantastical, and magnificent frames ever," says Prescott. "They were intended as over-door panels in a French hotel decorated in the rococo taste with chinoiserie accoutrements."

The print room adjoining the main dining room, used to accommodate additional guests during large parties, was also inspired by the Dunbars' travels. Intrigued by the print room they saw in Castletown when touring Ireland with Desmond Guinness, they took a "print-room- and grotto-seeking expedition" with their friend Gervaise Jackson-Stopps. "We even discovered an early American print room in the colonial town of Portsmouth, New Hampshire," they recall. The couple hired preeminent designer Nicola Wingate-Saul to create a print room for their summer home on Cape Cod. Prescott, having learned the collage-like technique of applying prints surrounded by intricate borders and flourishes to painted walls, created this vermilion room with Dutch and French engravings as a surprise for his wife.

Antique French hand-blocked and collaged scenic wallpaper covers the walls of the large dining room next door. Made circa 1790, during the height of Europe's fascination with Pompeii and Herculaneum, the wallpaper depicts a famous image of an incense burner, architectural forms, and classical motifs found in the wall paintings of the cities' ancient villas. The Dunbars' passion for early American furniture and art is also expressed in this room, where their Philadelphia Chippendale highboy dominates one end and a 1785 Virginia huntboard stands against another. A portrait of Prescott's great-grandaunt, painted in New Orleans by French expatriate artist Jean-Joseph Vaudechamps, hangs above the mantel.

German Expressionist artwork, much of it purchased by Sarah's mother during art studies in Munich in 1933, adds yet more diversity to the objects arrayed throughout the house. These paintings hang in the living room above a rare pair of gilded George II tables, which are laden with treasures amassed over the years by various family members. The oldest of these are a group of Attic black- and red-figure pottery and sherds ranging in age from circa 540 to 425 B.C., acquired by Lander, who recently completed a masters degree in classical archaeology at Oxford University. The tables also hold a Steuben art nouveau glass lamp, a German carved boxwood panel, circa 1650, and a female head sculpted by German Expressionist artist Wilhelm Lehmbruck. "I put my collection of Attic pottery on this table because I always found the Lehmbruck, though expressionistic, to possess a classical notion of beauty, particularly her almond eyes and fleshy lips," Lander says.

LEFT Matthew Boulton candlesticks and a John Scoffield tureen adorn the dining room table beneath the glitter of a Regency chandelier. The delicate fretwork and scrolls of a fine 1765 highboy made in Philadelphia form an elegant silhouette against the colorful wallpaper.

RIGHT A 1785 Virginia huntboard Prescott inherited from his father displays the graceful curves of neoclassical American furniture. An extremely rare trio of boxes, two for knives and one for forks and spoons, is decorated with silver mountings and ball-and-claw feet.

OVERLEAF A mid-seventeenth-century German carved panel, a German Expressionist head of a woman, late Hellenistic and Roman terra-cotta heads, and Attic black-figure and red-figure pottery and fragments share a tabletop in the Dunbars' living room. Made from marble and semiprecious stones laid out in a geometric pattern, this specimen marble top adorns a George II table.

Adjoining the pink living room is a parlor with cobalt blue walls hung with portraits by American masters James Peale, John Singleton Copley, and Robert Salmon, as well as two watercolors by John James Audubon. The room's furnishings include a tea table made by mid-eighteenth-century Newport cabinetmakers Townsend and Goddard, which features rare articulated ball-and-claw feet and its original Vermont marble top. Surrounded by English George II chairs, this table frequently forms a gathering place for guests enjoying cocktails or after-dinner champagne. Meissen figures by Johann Kändler of turbaned potentates, one astride an elephant and the other, a rhinoceros, stand on the Greek Revival marble mantel. "It is most unusual to have a rhinoceros as a mantel garniture," says Prescott, pointing out that elephants are far more common.

In this house full of uncommon objects, there are two more rooms opening off the wide center hall that are filled with carefully chosen and cherished antiques. One is a library furnished with a pair of English library tables, circa 1770, that invite the perusal of books. The room is also enjoyed by gentleman guests who, in an anachronistic throwback to the nineteenth-century tradition, withdraw from the ladies' company to enjoy

FAR RIGHT Late eighteenth-century library desks with wide tops and shallow kneeholes stand back to back in the Dunbars' library. Contemporaneous English fabric decorates the room's walls and windows.

after-dinner cigars, brandy, and port. Eighteenth-century fabric that once draped the tall windows of an English country house upholsters the walls and windows of this masculine retreat. A gilded Cornelius and Company gasolier that originally graced the Dunbars' dining room illumines the room, which also contains a hidden bar filled with vintage cocktail paraphernalia.

On the far side of a staircase leading to the family's private chambers lies a guest bedroom with walls upholstered in bright gold damask. A sumptuous rococo bed made in Philadelphia and found for the Dunbars by antiquarian Roger Bacon dominates the room. Mr. Bacon, whose personal collecting began with high-style Americana but ended

LEFT First-edition prints from John Jay Audubon's elephant folio hang in the center hall of the Dunbars' Greek Revival house.

RIGHT Gold bed-hangings of custom-loomed French fabric, based on a Louis XV pattern, perfectly complement the ornate rococo bed made in Philadelphia.

with simpler Pilgrim furniture, prophesied the Dunbars' taste might change as well. "We said we doubted it," Mr. Dunbar recalls. Soon after that conversation, Mr. Bacon discovered this bed and called the Dunbars, announcing that he had found "the bed-of-all-beds, the most magnificent rococo bed he had ever seen."

Many museums would have been delighted to possess the high-style Chippendale bed, but the owner had expressly insisted that it be sold to a private collector. Now it adorns the Dunbars' guest bedroom, draped in gold silk damask hand-loomed in France and inspired by a swatch of Louis XV fabric. "I find it ironic that Roger told us that we would eventually want simpler and more austere furniture," Sarah comments. "If anything, our tastes have become more ornate and positively baroque."

Allure of the *Exotic*

This limited edition, published by the Folio Society, features illustrations of exotic flora and fauna by eighteenth-century Dutch artist and naturalist Maria Sibylla Merian. It is one of many rare volumes in the New Orleans library of Quinn Peeper and Michael Harold.

One of the defining characteristics of Southern style is a strong sense of place. Families often live for generations in the same town or ancestral home, finding immeasurable comfort amid familiar things. A bouquet of camellias blooming brightly, the scent of mahogany polished with beeswax, the softness of silk carpets laid across heart-pine floors—such pleasures furnish visions of classic Southern style in Williamsburg, Savannah, Natchez, and elsewhere. It is easy to be lulled by them into the popular misconception that the South is a sleepy, provincial place. The reality, however, is that the region has long been a global crossroads populated by well-traveled people with a taste for the exotic.

When the first settlers arrived in the Virginia, Carolina, Louisiana, and Georgia colonies, the sight of Spanish moss and alligators, wide rivers and swampy mudflats, broad oaks and towering pines was stirringly unfamiliar. Before long, these settlers began building homes inspired by English, French, and Spanish architecture in New World towns including Jamestown, Charleston, and New Orleans. To adapt European styles to their hot climate, early Southerners looked to the West Indies for inspiration, borrowing forms such as porches, galleries, and louvered shutters from Barbados, Jamaica, and Haiti (then known as San Domingue). The resulting dwellings, including Charleston's single houses and New Orleans' Creole cottages, reveal the global exchange of ideas that lies at the heart of Southern style.

Once the South's major port cities were firmly established, the region's residents were connected to an international trade economy offering access to design ideas and decorative objects from England, Europe, India, China, Japan, and beyond. The homes of wealthy nineteenth-century Southerners often boasted French cornice decorations made of *papier-mâché*, English furniture, Indian style fabrics, Chinese export ware, japanned furniture, and Italian artwork. These were arrayed in houses reflecting architectural influences derived from ancient Greece, Renaissance Italy, and, on occasion, Egypt.

Southerners today continue to express this fascination with the foreign. Commissioning hand-painted porcelain from China or building new homes inspired by West Indian plantations, some homeowners directly emulate their forebears. Others adopt the international spirit of Old South style, but expand its global reach, decorating rooms with textiles from Afghanistan, ceramics from Morocco, and zebra skins from Africa. Together, these Southerners weave a worldly cloth entwining the adventurous spirit of the region's early residents with the boldness of today's cosmopolitan South.

Indigo Dreams

HOUSE OF SUSAN AND TRENHOLM WALKER
CHARLESTON, SOUTH CAROLINA

*W*hen Susan and Trenholm Walker sought the perfect house to serve as a sanctuary for home life, a space for creative work, and a place for small community gatherings, they combed the streets of Charleston, South Carolina. The son of an ardent preservationist, Trenholm was drawn to the old dwellings of the historic city—beautiful survivors of time, storms, fires, wars, and reckless renovations. An artist and, with her husband, an impassioned participant in the city's artistic, spiritual, and political life, Susan wanted a house commodious enough for a studio as well as community events. When their search turned up a nineteenth-century Charleston single house with an inviting side porch and spacious double parlors, they knew they had found the right dwelling place for their dreams.

Compared to many of the city's architectural *grandes dames*, the house is not overburdened with the highly decorative cornice moldings, door surrounds, and mantels that characterize the Federal and Greek Revival styles. "The house has a simple grandeur," says Trenholm. "It doesn't use any special effects." Instead, it has what he describes as "wonderful signifiers of the past"—transom windows, the old servants' call bells that no longer work, and solid heart-pine pocket doors. Susan also loves these relics of the past, including ceiling medallions in the double parlors, from which old-fashioned ceiling fans hang. "People think we should have chandeliers there, but we love the nonchalance of drowsy fans ruffling the air."

Another aspect of the house that attracted Susan and Trenholm is its balance of large and intimate spaces. In addition to spacious entertaining rooms, the first floor also includes an airy nook at the end of the long side porch, which accommodates a home office, and an old-fashioned snuggery cozying up to an antique brick fireplace by the kitchen. While the couple liked the look of these inviting spaces for their private life, they also appreciated a gracious double parlor that provided the perfect space for entertaining small groups or large receptions.

Luxurious fabrics, including silk dupioni curtains and velvet upholstery, contrast with the natural textures of a sea-grass rug, zebra pelt, and old coral in the Walkers' front parlor. The room's tall French doors open onto a side porch, ushering in Charleston's balmy breezes.

The house's most illustrious resident, Charleston preservationist Susan Pringle Frost, hosted many meetings in these rooms. The founder of the Society for the Preservation of Old Buildings (now the Preservation Society of Charleston) in 1920, she was also a radical feminist, hosting female suffragist meetings in the house and a gathering of the National Woman's Party in 1915. "We want to return that vital pulse to this house by inviting people through our door who share our interest in historic preservation, environmental conservation, political activism, and the arts," Trenholm explains.

Susan, a textile artist whose work synthesizes the craftsmanship and symbolic nature of textiles from around the world, took on the task of weaving the couple's personal and political aspirations into an aesthetic setting. Naturally, textiles played a large role in the decor. In the front parlor, she combined new and old fabrics, including antique Berber wedding sashes from Morocco and a contemporary silk throw made by Laotian weavers for Lulan, a Charleston-based textile company. Highly textured pillows made from old Indian embroidery share space with lustrous dupioni silk curtains the shade of aged bourbon. Old Indian saris, a colorful bolster adorned with Afghani textile fragments, and a Turkmenistan wedding cloak, studded with old coins, add further embellishment.

A large Mexican bread bowl on the room's floor overflows with folded suzanis from Uzbekistan, their carefully stitched, colorful decoration contrasting with the bold black-and-white stripes of a zebra pelt. A souvenir of the couple's trip to Tanzania, where they climbed Mount Kilimanjaro, the pelt is one of several reminders of international travels. These also include a sculpture made of woven bark that they purchased in Oaxaca, which hangs above the mantel.

For the dining room, Susan designed a pair of narrow tables employing a Moroccan arch, a Chinese red lacquer surface, and narrow Shaker proportions. Depending upon the size and nature of gatherings, she places them end to end to create a long table, divides them into two separate tables, or places them side by side to form a square.

93

LEFT Susan and Trenholm opened up the second floor of the attached kitchen behind their house to create a spacious and luminous weaving studio. Charleston artisan Bob Hines fashioned the sconces, which are decorated with stencils based on antique Japanese kimonos.

RIGHT An arresting arrangement of objects populates a corner in Susan's studio, including an old container from an English textile mill, a striped Turkish blanket, and embroidered and appliquéd fabric fragments from Turkey. Old spindles, also found in Turkey, and a skein of linen yarn, freshly dyed with indigo and ready for Susan's loom, also grace the old brick hearth.

To create a neutral setting for these high-impact elements, Susan chose a creamy wall color with hints of amber. Simple falls of silk drape windows, which are also furnished with the louvered shutters Southerners have employed for centuries to control the flow of light and air. Comfortable furniture with unpatterned upholstery allows Susan to swap pillows and throws in response to the changing seasons: hot tones of red, gold, and saffron in winter and cool shades of turquoise and indigo in summer. Sea grass, leather, coral, and carved wood add more texture to the mix, blending the elegant with the organic.

Pocket doors separate the front parlor from the dining room. After intimate before-dinner drinks in the living room, Susan loves the drama of throwing open the pocket doors to the dining room, with its red lacquer tables shimmering with candles and flowers. A magnificent Adras robe from Uzbekistan, mounted like butterfly wings on canvas, hangs above an upright piano upon which she often accompanies impromptu singing gatherings. Above the fireplace opposite, an appliquéd piece from India unfurls over the mantel, which holds green-glazed pottery from China and blue-and-white ceramics from Fez.

The cinnabar-colored tables stand end to end in the middle of the room, flanked by matching lacquered benches topped with gold, suede-like cushions. Designed by Susan, and fabricated by Charleston woodworker Walter Biffle, the tables merge Chinese and Moroccan style, with a touch of American Shaker influence. "Walter told me that these tables, which measure twenty-nine inches, are the same width as Shaker tables," she explains. As a result, the tables (and the backless benches surrounding them) invite diners to lean in towards one another during conversation.

In addition to these double parlors, which are common in old Charleston houses, the dwelling offers an uncommon chamber hidden in the back of the property. In the old kitchen house, once a separate structure, the couple created a soaring, two-story studio for Susan. An office occupies the upper floor of the space, with a spiral staircase that descends to the ground level, where Susan's loom stands before the old brick fireplace. As elsewhere in the house, both symbolism and utility are interlaced in this space. "I weave on the hearth, at the level of the earth," says Susan. "I write at my desk which is directly above the loom, reflecting upon the weaving that takes place below. This creates an axis for my work." The arrangement also yields a two-story wall upon which Susan can hang large works in progress, as well as finished pieces, which she displays during open-studio receptions.

LEFT Shelves in Susan's studio hold a trove of textile-related objects including embroidered caps from Turkey, old shuttles from closed mills in South Carolina, embroidery and mirrorwork from India, Kuba raffia cloth from the Congo, antique vestments from Europe, and a quilt that had been hand-sewn by her great-grandmother before she had turned thirteen.

RIGHT Compared to the brightly colored decor of the rooms below, the master bedroom is muted and more simply adorned. "I wanted a quieter place at the beginning and end of the day—a chance for renewal amid pure, serene simplicity," Susan explains.

The renovated kitchen house also includes a tiny cave of a space behind the brick chimney where Susan stores textile objects she has collected, as well as skeins and cones of yarn that await her weaving. These include strands of cotton dyed with indigo, the vibrant blue dye extracted from the indigo plant indigenous to the South Carolina low country. First produced successfully for international trade by a female plantation owner, Eliza Lucas Pinckney, the natural blue dye is Susan's new favorite. One of her recent works features an 8 by 8-foot robe of indigo-dyed cotton and silk embellished with small saffron-colored pieces. These are woven with symbols of her journey as a Southern woman, an artist, a traveler, and an activist. While this piece is two-dimensional, the house where it was made is a three-dimensional weaving of this couple's life, loves, and passions.

East of Eton

HOUSE OF QUINN PEEPER AND MICHAEL HAROLD
NEW ORLEANS, LOUISIANA

The screen of gold-on-cerulean silk in Quinn Peeper's bedroom was designed by Rosemary James for her company, Faulkner House Designs. Arranged on a nearby tabletop, a costume hat from the Ballets Russe, turquoise worry beads from Greece, and classical busts hint at the global range of objects displayed throughout the house.

When Quinn Peeper attended Oxford University, many of his British classmates spent between-term vacations in India. The American abroad, however, preferred to explore the European continent, from Paris to St. Petersburg. "I hadn't seen everything I wanted to see in Europe," says the Tennessee-born doctor who now resides in New Orleans. "So why would I travel to India?" But India-mania hit soon after, when Quinn returned from Oxford to complete his medical training at Columbia University. Signing up for several months' residency in India, he lived in Rajastan and traveled extensively. "I bought carved ivories, painted miniatures, prints of the British Raj, bronze figures of Ganesh and Shiva, polo mallets, whips, and anything else I could pack," he recalls.

Although Michael Harold is equally well traveled, he is not quite so obsessively acquisitive. "When I was growing up, anybody and anything that was foreign fascinated me," says Michael, a lawyer and native New Orleanian. "When I began traveling in earnest, I tended to acquire stories and languages more than things." However, Michael does plead guilty to going to charity balls in New Orleans (the pair serves on boards of several organizations including the New Orleans Opera) and coming home with unexpected silent auction items, including an antique French dining table and chairs.

When Quinn moved to New Orleans to practice medicine, he recalls: "I thought I was finally going to decorate my house with all the English things I wanted." But then he met interior designer Rosemary James (co-owner of Faulkner House Books and founder of New Orleans' Words & Music literary festival), and all that changed. "Rosemary and I share a love of literature," says Quinn, who serves on the Faulkner House board with Michael. "She reminds me of Elsie de Wolfe, the way she combines stripes and leopard print, old mirrors and things with patina, history, and whimsy." Rosemary is also a determined Francophile, not just because she loves the look of Louis XV and Louis XVI furniture, but also because it works so well in the scale of French Quarter dwellings.

LEFT A collection of antique opera glasses attests to Quinn and Michael's love of music. A silver maté cup purchased during travels in Argentina adds an exotic touch to the tabletop composition.

RIGHT Prints of classical subjects and portrait miniatures of Quinn and Michael by Thomas Sully III flank pocket doors leading to the entrance hall. A tall Directoire-style chair upholstered in vintage Fortuny stripes and a Louis XVI chair covered with a Bergamo damask offer stylish seating for guests during after-dinner piano concerts.

When Quinn met Rosemary, he lived in the French Quarter, and the delicate furnishings she recommended looked right at home. Now, two houses later, Quinn has moved uptown to a more spacious Queen Anne–style house, circa 1903, in a part of town first inhabited by English and American settlers. Here, the French pieces Quinn purchased a decade earlier share a gracious suite of entertaining rooms with Italian paintings and Grand Tour intaglios and porcelains, Chinese export ware armorial china, a Swedish chandelier, art deco club chairs, and contemporary metal furniture designed by New Orleanian Mario Villa.

The Italian paintings and decorative objects are the spoils of collecting sprees enjoyed between master classes in piano the two have attended annually in Tolentino, in the Le Marche region of Italy. Both Quinn and Michael are prize-wining pianists who have performed at Carnegie Hall and other major American venues. Whiling away the nervous hours before a Carnegie Hall recital with Rosemary at New York's D&D Building, Quinn purchased the marble and plaster plaques that flank his bed from antiques dealer and designer John Roselli.

Quinn and Michael's collection also includes period Grand Tour intaglios—bas-relief classical images made in Italy as souvenirs for American tourists in the late eighteenth and nineteenth centuries. Hanging in the library, an inviting room glazed a brilliant shade of vermilion, the intaglios are greatly outnumbered by Quinn and Michael's books, which range from first editions of the Cecil Beaton diaries to collectible editions by P. G. Wodehouse and Ian Fleming. A recent addition to their acquisitions is a limited-edition reproduction of a volume published in 1705 of illustrations by Dutch artist and naturalist Maria Sibylla Merian depicting exotic flora and fauna in Surinam.

While much of the furniture in the living room is demurely French, the bold stripes on a pair of Louis XVI wing chairs, oversize gilded cornices, and an amber-toned Agra carpet add ballast to the mix. Large round tables placed in corners hold more of the pair's collections. One table is covered with an array of opera glasses, which Quinn, an opera lover, calls "Peeper's peepers." Another holds a combination of silver maté cups from Argentina and antique-horn snuff mills, an item that, Quinn points out, was also collected by Diana Vreeland. Bronze and porcelain figures from Greek and Roman antiquity contribute a note of classical gravity to the tabletop arrangements.

A gracious staircase leads from an entrance hall spacious enough to accommodate a Baldwin grand piano to the second floor. On this floor, the pair's fascination with things both Western and Eastern is clearly demonstrated. While the hall is hung with Quinn's collection of aquatints from Richard Ackerman's early nineteenth-century

A pair of art deco chairs upholstered in a Kravet leopard print adds a touch of early twentieth-century glamour to the library, which is glazed a brilliant shade of vermilion. Early editions fill the custom-made shelves of the room, which opens onto an enclosed porch.

portfolio of scenes from Oxford University, the guest room is decorated with objects from India. Although the four-poster bed is a traditional Southern rice bed, a Kashmiri shawl Quinn inherited from his great-grandmother (who also owned the bed) covers its foot. Twelve prints depicting the British regiments in India during the Raj period hang on the walls, along with a selection of Indian miniatures on ivory and paper. A period campaign desk purchased in the Cotswolds during a trip the two took with Lady Henrietta Spencer-Churchill adds another Anglo-Indian touch to the room.

The aura of genteel restraint that characterizes the entertaining rooms is abandoned in the master suite, where gold silk cascades from a gilded corona, forming a canopy above a bed piled high with pillows. Designed by Rosemary after an iron fence detail, the corona incorporates the Greek key motif. Rosemary also designed the chandelier, which is embellished with giant glass baubles blown at the New Orleans Glass Works. Quinn

LEFT A service of armorial porcelain produced in a Chinese factory by de Gournay brings to mind the table settings created for the English and American well-to-do by the British East India Company. Quinn's heraldic arms, which feature piano keys and a stork holding a cotton boll, reflect his personal history and interests.

RIGHT A Swedish chandelier and Louis XVI dining room chairs add delicate grace notes to the masculine elegance of the dining room. In addition to his armorial porcelain service, silver with Quinn's crest was produced by James Robinson in New York after an antique design.

A French chair, a pair of classical relief sculptures from antiques dealer John Roselli, a Venetian mask, and a headboard and corona designed by Rosemary James with a Greek key motif create a cosmopolitan montage in Quinn's bedroom.

LEFT Quinn's habit of collecting Anglo-Indian objects has continued well beyond the time of his elective studies in India during medical school. While this period campaign desk was purchased recently in the Cotswolds, the polo mallets leaning against the wall next to it are spoils of earlier collecting sprees.

RIGHT In the Raj room, as Quinn and Michael have named this guest bedroom, nineteenth-century prints of the British regiments serving in colonial India decorate the walls. An antique Kashmiri shawl belonging to Quinn's great-grandmother attests to the popularity of Indian textiles in the Victorian South.

and Michael selected the classical bust that broods near the bedside table and the marble head of a muse that presides over the master bath.

In yet another invocation of the English fascination with things from the East, Quinn recently commissioned a service of armorial porcelain from de Gournay. Just as in centuries past the British East India Company employed Chinese factories to produce porcelains blending Asian decoration with English shapes, so de Gournay produces Chinese export ware today. Working with de Gournay's designers, Quinn created place settings and serving pieces decorated with his heraldic arms. Featuring the keys of a piano and a stork holding a cotton boll, the heraldry reflects his passion for piano, his profession as an obstetrician, and his family's background in cotton. Quinn also commissioned sterling silverware with the same crest from James Robinson in New York. In fine English tradition, he and Michael inaugurated the tableware with a dinner party for the New Orleans chapter of the Anglo-Indian Sporting and Dining Club, followed by an informal concert on the grand piano. Although the accents of the party were Southern, the spirit of the evening was pure Raj quartet.

New Orleans Polyrhythms

HOUSE OF ANN AND TIM KOERNER: NEW ORLEANS, LOUISIANA

A view from the living room of Ann and Tim Koerner's New Orleans residence offers insight into Ann's sophisticated design aesthetic. Owner of Ann Koerner Antiques, the designer enjoys combining a global array of antique and modern pieces. The bold geometries and homespun textures of the living room's African reed rug and the dining room's Indian Dhurrie contrast with refined nineteenth-century saber-leg chairs surrounding the English pedestal table. Leavening the room's otherwise formal furnishings, a Diego Giacometti chandelier with irregular coral-like branches injects a touch of whimsy.

ew Orleans . . . resembles no other city on the face of the earth, yet it recalls vague memories of a hundred cities. It owns suggestions of towns in Italy, and in Spain, of cities in England and in Germany, of seaports in the Mediterranean, and of seaports in the tropics." So wrote one of New Orleans' most impassioned chroniclers, Lafcadio Hearn. A first-generation American with a seafaring Irish father and a Greek mother, this nineteenth-century writer was well qualified to describe the city's international society. He is also a favored author of Ann and Tim Koerner, Southerners who bring together in their heritage, their home, and their businesses many strands of the city's complex culture.

Tim's family came from Germany in the mid-nineteenth century to settle in New Orleans, where they became suppliers of baking goods and ingredients. Ann grew up in Mississippi, in a farmhouse filled with African textiles and tribal objects collected by her father. A botanist, he spent several years growing rubber trees in Africa before settling in Mississippi. Ann's mother was the daughter of an old Polish shipping family whose early childhood in Nicaragua and Germany informed her taste and her work as an artist. "Objects, art, and textiles from all the places my parents lived filled our home," recalls Ann, "leading to an early multicultural awareness for me and my siblings."

A dealer and decorator who operates Ann Koerner Antiques in a converted double-shotgun house on Magazine Street, Ann reflects that "most of the things I'm drawn to in my work and my own decor are linked to my childhood influences and family history." Tim, who runs the family business importing gourmet baking and culinary products, travels frequently to Europe, where Ann joins him for buying trips in Paris and Italy. The bounty of these shopping expeditions yields not only a shop inventory of European antiques and international items from the International Homestyle Exhibition in Paris, but also decorative objects for their new home.

Before Hurricane Katrina, the couple lived in Pass Christian, Mississippi, in a spacious shoreside cottage that was ravaged, along with most of its contents, by the storm's wind and ocean surge. Soon after the storm, they purchased a charming turn-of-the-nineteenth-century house with Doric columns and a shady porch in New Orleans' "Uptown" district. Surrounded by gardens, and organized with a floor plan giving several rooms triple exposures, the house is filled with light. On one side, a formal garden offers up the scent of old roses, and on the other, a dense stand of bamboo sways in the breeze, lending an exotic, tropical mood. "This is the kind of contrast that every New Orleanian loves," says Tim.

Marrying their global sense of style with a Southern love of warm, inviting, and personal spaces, the Koerners began life anew in this house. The front door opens into an inviting living room, where Ann's relaxed way of combining varied textures, styles, periods, and nationalities finds full expression. In the living room, an eighteenth-century English armchair lies hidden beneath a linen slipcover, its soft form contrasting with the crisp outlines of a painted French wooden bench, circa 1875. Fabric from John Robshaw covers the bench's cushions, its bold stripes creating dynamic interplay with an African rug's zigzagging pattern of leather and reeds.

A 1960s clear acrylic table adds more geometric verve to the room while injecting a very unexpected material. And a carved wooden table from Burma, with fulsome, vegetative lines and distressed green paint, lends an organic quality to the mix. By painting the walls a calming ochre-like beige and keeping her window treatments simple, using canvas Roman shades, Ann created a soothing, blank page upon which these ingredients write their own story.

Ann and Tim Koerner's late nineteenth-century cottage has pristine Beaux-Arts-style decorations, including fluted Doric columns and an entablature decorated with floral garlands. However, the small jungle of tall bamboo that sways and clatters in the breeze beside the house lends the dwelling a slightly exotic, tropical air.

LEFT The scroll arm of a nineteenth-century French bench offers curvaceous contrast to the rhythmic diamond pattern of a contemporary African rug made of woven reeds and leather. The crisp stripes of a John Robshaw textile contribute neat lines to the mix.

RIGHT Above a rustic Swedish cabinet hangs a painting of a Lake Ponchartrain beach scene, by New Orleans artist George Dereau, circa 1960. A tiny African figure on the cabinet, an eighteenth-century Italian side chair, and a Burmese table reflect Ann's freewheeling approach to style.

While most of the objects in the room are new acquisitions, they share space with a few highly prized possessions rescued from their old home. Among these is a painting by family friend George Dereau depicting Lincoln Beach, a now-defunct water park on Lake Ponchartrain popular with New Orleans' African-American population. The couple was also able to salvage a small portion of their books about art, architecture, and history. Although all the volumes on the lower shelves of their Mississippi home were damaged by the storm surge, they salvaged the remainder of their books and arranged them in shelves built into their new living room's wall.

These shelves flank a large, arched opening framing a view of the dining room, which employs the same color of paint and window treatment as the living room. Here, a simple English pedestal table, made in the late eighteenth century, offers a restrained centerpiece around which more highly decorative elements are arrayed. A painted iron

chandelier designed by Diego Giacometti that resembles interlaced branches of coral hangs above the table, adding an irregular, organic shape to the room. Fornasetti plates, blown Venetian glass tumblers, and a sea-urchin-like Italian glass bowl in a brilliant shade of citrine contribute color and pattern to the mix.

"What I love about Italian design is the way these pieces balance a sense of play with a highly refined design sensibility," says Ann. "They add a touch of the unexpected in formal interiors and a jolt of high design in an informal one." According to Tim, who is the historian in the family, decorating with Italian objects makes perfect sense in New Orleans because Italians formed one of the largest immigrant populations in the city. Combined with the English dining table—a reminder of the English merchants who immigrated to New Orleans in the nineteenth century—the room's furnishings create a kind of anthropological collage.

LEFT Chairs and a gilded mirror made in America, circa 1820, lend traditional elegance to the dining room. Venetian glass, including a prickly vessel and colorful tumblers, and gilded Fornasetti plates add lively energy, while Ann's serious self-portrait and a vase made by her friend Gail Keenan, recently deceased, contribute gravitas.

RIGHT Ann was drawn to this early nineteenth-century, high-style Empire New York console for several reasons. "My paternal forbears were founders of New Haven, Connecticut, and I find myself loving early furniture made in the Northeast," she explains. She also couldn't resist its exaggerated lion's paws and Corinthian capitals.

OVERLEAF An aquatint of Boston's harbor hangs above the bed in the master bedroom. Another international port, Boston's wharves received a great deal of Chinese imports, including rolls of Canton matting like these floor coverings. The andirons on the trunk were made from African statues belonging to Ann's father.

On one wall, an antique print of the Mississippi River, seen from the roof of the Customs House in the French Quarter, pays homage to the port, which was the largest point of embarkation in America in the early nineteenth century. "Coming from an old shipping family," says Ann, "I find I am drawn to port scenes." The print hangs above an exquisite marble-topped console with robust lion's paw feet, columns with gold Corinthian capitals that look a bit like palm fronds, and intricate ormolu garniture. The high-style Empire piece was made in New York, circa 1820, and immediately appealed to Ann's refined design sensibility when she discovered it in an antiques market. "I love the bold shapes and the patina of the old materials," say Ann, who chose a striped blue-and-white dhurrie rug to balance the console's formal character.

In the bedroom, Ann created a simple retreat with a headboard-free bed ("I find you don't need one if the other design elements are strong," she opines.) surmounted by a large port scene of Boston. Uncomplicated chairs with canvas slipcovers positioned beside windows provide delightfully snug spots for reading. A painted country chest holding textiles she has collected from around the world stands at the bed's foot and supports a pair of andirons made from African statues collected by Ann's father. After having somehow passed out of family ownership, the andirons resurfaced in the home of a New Orleans acquaintance. Longing to have these reminders of her childhood home in her own house, she persuaded the friend to sell them back to her.

With so many cultures and periods represented throughout the rooms, and a poignant backstory of loss and new beginnings, the decoration of the house bears some resemblance to the jazz music that was born in New Orleans. Whether played slowly in the city's famed funeral parades or jauntily in honky-tonks, jazz brings together African and Caribbean beats, European musical instruments, and a sensual Southern joie de vivre. These same rich polyrhythms find expression in this Uptown New Orleans home, where two Southerners improvised a new life, blending together the many strands of their past and the cultures of the city they both love.

The Illusion of Grandeur

PIED-À-TERRE OF TOM LEDDY: SAVANNAH, GEORGIA

Iron Egyptian gates mounted
with bronze lions, a reference
to Tom Leddy's zodiacal sign,
open into his salon, where a
tiger pelt spreads out beneath
a cast-stone French garden
table. Cast from a wood original, the table has the appearance of grain and a wonderful
patina that appealed to Tom.

The restrained Savannah gray-brick facade of Tom Leddy's late nineteenth-century townhouse gives no hint of the opulence that lies behind it. Standing in a row of identical, attached townhouses radiating off Troupe Square—one of Savannah's quietest urban gardens—it is a modest structure in ornamentation and scale. The front doors of this row of residences are at street level, unlike most Savannah houses, where the main entrances are usually raised well above the street, requiring residents and visitors to climb steep stairs to enter. In addition to offering the interior some protection from occasional floodwaters, this raised-level arrangement creates a sense of drama, gradually elevating guests to the level of the grand entertaining rooms.

At Tom's house, there is no such prelude. The experience of opening the front door is no less dramatic than the awakening of Jonathan Swift's Gulliver to find himself in the land of Lilliputians. But while Gulliver discovered a strange land where everything was small, inside Tom's house, everything seems bigger, grander, and more extravagant than the world outside the door. In truth, the townhouse's rooms are smaller than those of the finest Savannah houses, but the sense of scale and grandeur they impart is akin to that of European villas and palaces. "You don't need a great deal of square footage to create the illusion of opulence and space," Tom says.

Although the house has only 2,900 square feet of interior space, it has high ceilings, plentiful windows, and wonderful light. These attractions, plus the fact that most historical interior details had been erased in an aggressive 1960s remodeling, allowed Tom and a team of experts to create a fantastical Italianate interior, channeling the baroque excesses of Old Venice. "I think Savannah and Venice have something in common," says Tom. "Venice, to me, is a total fantasy land. And so is Savannah, with all the beautiful, old buildings and garden squares. Like Savannah, Venice had a poor period, but while it lasted four hundred years, Savannah's only lasted a century. Hard times actually saved both cities, because there was little money to tear down old things and build new ones."

The drawing room floor, originally plain pine, was embellished with a swirling geometric pattern adapted from an eighteenth-century Florentine palazzo. Exquisite silk valences worthy of windows overlooking the Grand Canal were made by Virginia Di Sciascio, using embroidery rescued from fraying eighteenth-century curtains.

A Fortuny lamp, an Egyptoid
chair, and a French daybed
painted in eighteenth-century
Russian style add to the
drawing room's mood of
exotic opulence. Cushions
upholstered with Christopher
Highland cut velvet add more
pattern and luster to the piece.

From early childhood onward, Tom traveled a great deal in Europe, including trips to Venice—experiences that shaped his taste as an adult. "My parents, who lived in Philadelphia, were very into brown, English furniture," he recalls. "Nothing else would do. To me, the idea of a residence that reflects a fantasy, far away from your everyday world, appealed so much more." Working in New York's fast-paced investment field, Tom enjoys creating getaway homes where he can escape and relax with family and friends. "I chose Savannah this time because I wanted a place with architectural history, where I could walk around in a beautiful setting."

But now that Tom has completed the transformation of his Savannah retreat into a fantastical setting evoking what he calls "the insanely, otherworldly beauty of Venice," he doesn't even want to get out and walk around. Just sitting in his garden, or the small salons and balcony that overlook it, satisfies his wanderlust. "More than any other place, Venice is where I long to be. If you have a good trompe l'oeil painter, you can be in your house and go anywhere in the world," says Tom.

This magical transportation takes place the moment the front door opens to an entrance hall overlooking the dining room, which is crowned with a ceiling painted to resemble decorated coffers and a sky-blue dome. A large Venetian glass chandelier hangs from the center of the "dome," glittering with candlelight by night. By day, sunlight glows through windows draped with gold Rubelli silk from Venice. The room's walls are decorated with vistas combining elements of Italian and coastal Georgia landscapes, framed with painted drapery swags that imitate the Venetian silk. In one wall, an antique wood door opens into the kitchen beneath a trompe l'oeil arch of hand-molded plaster with a baroque shell motif.

The next element that commands attention is the floor of hand-cut stone. "There is nothing that creates a sense of old worldliness better than antique stone," says Tom, who had this eighteenth-century stone floor shipped over from Portugal, along with two craftsmen to install it. The rustic texture of the stone and robust architectural painting contrast with the sheer, nearly weightless Venetian glass goblets and bud vases that adorn a dining table set with flower-like hues and forms. Gilded candelabra, gold-plated silverware, and place settings mixing several patterns and colors complete the scene. "When you entertain," says Thomas, "it's a form of theater, and the whole thing has to be great: the ambiance, the food, the conversation."

During parties, guests pass this room—a hint of things to come—as they climb stairs to the second-floor drawing room, the house's most dizzying chamber of delights. A floor of faux parquet creates an almost disorienting swirl of shape and shadow in a cavernous room, where time and space seem to dissolve, inviting visitors to imagine themselves in Venice, Versailles, or imperial Vienna. For the walls and ceilings, Tom and his decorative painter, Joseph Steiert of Palm Beach, created a pastiche of elements from Venetian palazzos, including a colorful palette of faux marble panels and columns, gilding, and polychrome wood.

Within this room, an eclectic collection of furnishings and objects creates an impression of decadent Old Europe, rather than a faithful re-creation of any specific place or period. A monumental eighteenth-century Italian neoclassical tapestry hangs between the

Antique stone flooring from Portugal and trompe l'oeil painting imitating carved and gilded wood, silk draperies, and garden scenes create an opulent fantasy world in Tom Leddy's Savannah dining room. Beneath a gossamer blown-glass chandelier from Venice, a seventeenth-century French table gleams with vermeil candelabra and colorful Venetian stemware.

room's two fireplaces. A pair of wood and iron chandeliers, circa 1920, is thought to have once graced the ballroom of a New York hotel. A curved art deco sofa salvaged from an ocean liner faces it. Tom had the sofa's woodwork sandblasted to achieve an antique pati-na, and hired textile artist Virginia Di Sciascio of Antique Textiles in New York to con-sult upon the selection and decoration of upholstery and pillows. His decorative painter created a similar sleight of hand by painting a French daybed shaped like a gondola with pale blue, ivory, and gold detail, thus transforming it into an elegant piece in the style of late eighteenth-century Russia.

To divide the long drawing room from a small salon behind it that overlooks the gar-den, Tom used one of his favorite architectural devices. "Almost every house I've had has some kind of outdoor gates used on the inside," he says. "They serve to separate the rooms without blocking the view or the light." Between these two rooms, Tom placed an

LEFT An allée of palm trees creates an illusion of increased scale in the small garden. While the symmetry of the garden and the classical statue hearken to traditional Italian garden design, French bistro furniture introduces a more modern and casual element.

RIGHT A pair of nineteenth-century Moors with oars in their hands and gondolas at their feet flanks a Venetian mirror in the guest bedroom. A brass and velvet corona that originally adorned a church sacristy now crowns a nine-teenth-century Italian bed decorated with wrought gold and silver.

art deco iron Egyptian gate embellished with bronze lion heads. Providing tantalizing glimpses of the salon, where a cast-cement French table rests atop a Bengal tiger pelt, the gates also throws shadows upon the drawing room's faux parquet floors.

With chairs arranged around a backgammon table, armchairs ideal for reading or watching a concealable plasma television, and a jasmine-covered balcony, the intimate salon is a favored afternoon and evening haunt. In the mornings, however, Tom prefers the garden room, a small chamber on the first floor that opens onto the courtyard behind the house. While walls of books on either side of the room invite perusal, the room's intense decor—eighteenth-century Portuguese tiles, painted ceiling beams, faux terrazzo floors, and a mélange of European furniture—steals the show.

In contrast to the decorative intensity of the interior, the garden offers a serene retreat. In keeping with Italian garden traditions, this space is symmetrical, with glossy green plants arrayed around an allée, terminating with a fountain. Despite the garden's small size (it is only 27 feet long), Tom was able to squeeze in three palm trees on either side to establish the allée, as well as a 9-foot-tall marble Italian sculpture that towers above the courtyard. Rather than emphasize the smallness of the garden, these elements visually increase the sense of space.

"The clever thing about this place is that there are elements throughout the design that bring the tone back down to earth," says Tom, pointing to the French bistro table in the garden's center as an example. "Not all the furniture is Venetian, or baroque in style, and a lot of it is stuff I had made. I'm not trying to fool anyone. But the house does have an opulence that has the power to transport you to some other place and time, which for me is Venice."

Memories of Xanadu

HOUSE OF ANN AND DAVID SILLIMAN: CHARLESTON, SOUTH CAROLINA

In the entrance hall of Ann and David Silliman's house, hand-cast European terra-cotta urns sit on American card tables, circa 1800, made in Massachusetts. Within the library, the combination of a European bronze urn, an American pedestal table, and an African zebra skin typifies the whimsical eclecticism Ann brings to the house's decor.

*W*hether sailing with family and friends or taking buying expeditions for Antiques of the Indies, their shop in Charleston, South Carolina, David and Ann Silliman travel frequently to the West Indies. Fascinated by the intermarriage of European and Caribbean style found in the architecture and furniture of the islands, the Sillimans decided to build a new home that expressed this hybrid style. When they discussed the project with Charleston-based architect Randolph Martz, they showed him photographs of Xanadu, a Cuban estate that once belonged to David's family. Although he had never visited the villa (it was appropriated by Castro in the 1950s and turned into a diplomatic retreat), David cherished his old photos of it, including one of his grandfather standing near a long veranda enjoying a Cuban cigar.

When Randolph, who is an expert in classical architecture, saw the pictures, he noted parallels between the Caribbean villa and the dwellings of Pompeii and Herculaneum. "These were resort destinations for wealthy Romans, who built dwellings where they enjoyed the temperate climate and views of the sea," the architect explains. Working with the Sillimans, Randolph designed a house combining Pompeian details, including colonnades and courtyard-like spaces, with West Indian verandas and French doors.

To enter the house, one passes through a Roman-style colonnade to approach a pair of mahogany and glass doors. These open into a foyer where a wall of mahogany and glass, with French doors set in the middle, frames views of the library. Within this room, the warm tone of red-brown mahogany moldings contrasts with cool blue-tinted plaster walls. A zebra skin layered atop a grass rug adds casual, naturalistic elements that contrast with highly refined antiques, including a late eighteenth-century table and matched pedestals with Egyptoid caryatids. According to the Sillimans, these attest to England and France's early nineteenth-century fascination with Egypt—an interest that reflected their African colonial ambitions.

ABOVE While the house's wide porches and low-slung profile are reminiscent of Caribbean villas, the organization of symmetrical porches flanking a pergola reveals architect Randolph Martz's interest in Roman forms.

RIGHT In the library, French archaeological engravings of Egyptian artifacts hang above a pair of nineteenth-century pedestals with gilded and ebonized Egyptian caryatids. A taxidermied bobcat adds a dramatic touch of the wild in the family room next door.

Charleston artisan Gale Ray tinted the dining room's plaster with blue lime wash, then brushed it with six layers of various tones of brown to get a deep glow. Antique furnishings with simple silhouettes, including an American chest-on-frame, an Italian trestle table, and Caribbean caned chairs, create an unfussy dining room decor.

To the right of this room stretches the dwelling's largest space, a long living room Randolph describes as "the soul of the house." With 14-foot ceilings, weighty mahogany baseboards and cornices, and a fireplace of coral stone and mahogany, the room was designed to have what Randolph calls "early American, British colonial proportions." It easily accommodates large-scale furnishings including an ornate bull's-eye mirror and a tall cotton factor's desk made in Tennessee, circa 1815–1820. Mixed in with these American pieces, a Jamaican caned chaise and a planter's chair impart an air of languor to the room. "We love to mix centuries and countries," says Ann, who also collects items from the natural world, including animal pelts, mounted heads, antique ivory, and turtle shells. The granddaughter of a furrier, she is quick to point out that nothing was acquired illegally, including the zebra skins and kudu heads. These were acquired through government-sanctioned herd management practices or during the 1920s and '30s era of big-game hunting.

In the dining room next door, French doors in two walls open to porches, inviting cool evening breezes and the sound of a fountain. A rustic Italian trestle table, circa 1820, provides a perfect foil for two sets of West Indian caned chairs. One set from Martinique, made around 1815, has caned seats and backs in a klismos style popular during the French Directoire period. The other set, from St. Croix, has caned backs with a square silhouette associated with English styles.

A doorway from the dining room leads to a kitchen where an eighteenth-century Italian chandelier hangs from an exposed beam, casting a country farmhouse-like glow on terra-cotta-colored walls. Like all the walls in the house, these are covered with a skim coat of plaster and tinted lime wash that creates a depth of color difficult to achieve with paint. From the kitchen, a pair of French doors opens to a veranda spanning the rear of the house. Inspired by a Caribbean villa they visited, the Sillimans asked Randolph to create a porch covered with a translucent roof of oiled canvas. "I love the sound when the wind blows the canvas," says Ann. "It reminds me of canvas awnings in coastal Italy and the Caribbean." The veranda's floor of lignum vitae, an exotic hardwood, creates a dusky glow underfoot, contrasting with olive green plaster walls. French art deco bamboo chairs and rattan ceiling fans complete the indolent tropical atmosphere.

The variety of ceiling heights in the first-floor rooms, ranging from the living room's 14 feet to the family room's 8½ feet, creates a dynamic arrangement of rooms and hallways on the bedroom floor. "The floors go up and down, with steps climbing over various ceiling heights, to create a bedroom level that is fun to inhabit," says Randolph. Each bedroom opens onto a sun-drenched hallway where plentiful windows bring in light and air.

The Sillimans' master suite includes a bedroom and, on a lower level, a pair of dressing rooms and master bath. While the bathroom is equipped with luxuriously modern accoutrements, the bedroom is dominated by a large early nineteenth-century bed from the West Indies. Both headboard and footboard are pierced, to improve the flow of breezes for cool sleeping on steamy Caribbean nights. The carvings of crosses and rosettes, though finely executed, reflect the slightly eccentric quality of design that the Sillimans admire in high-style West Indian and Southern antiques. "Sometimes there is a quirky artisanship that gives a piece a sense of character, whimsy, and local flavor that distinguishes it from an English or European antecedent," Ann explains.

A carved rosewood planter's chair from the West Indies, circa 1830, contrasts with the highly refined rococo design of this circa 1770 secretary desk inherited by David. Ann's grandfather, a furrier, collected many of the animal skins in the house, including this giraffe pelt.

RIGHT A large Cuban bed with lions' paw feet and pierced headboard and footboard dominates the master bedroom. Pieces of late eighteenth- or early nineteenth-century English needlepoint hang on either side of the bed. Designed to cover church kneelers, they reiterate the religious references of the bed, which is decorated with carved crosses.

OPPOSITE A ceiling of oiled canvas creates soft light that bathes the long veranda behind the Sillimans' house. A painting by Michael Christie hangs above the mahogany and coral stone mantel of the fireplace, which makes the space a pleasant year-round gathering place.

It is this ability to discern such subtle qualities and the passion to decipher them that define a connoisseur. "When you start to learn about antiques," says David, "what is even more interesting than the object itself is the story behind the object: who owned it, who made it, what they had to go through to make it." Whether intentionally or not, the connoisseurs who created this house encoded it thoroughly with "character, whimsy, and local flavor." The result is a new house that is steeped in tradition, yet utterly timeless. "I once had a visitor ask me, 'How long did it take you to restore this place?'" says Ann. "It was the best kind of compliment we could get."

Charleston Bricolage

HOUSE OF AMELIA HANDEGAN: CHARLESTON, SOUTH CAROLINA

The word *eclectic* is often used to describe rooms where furnishings and objets d'art from disparate periods and nations share space. In reference to the aesthetic of Southern tastemaker Amelia Handegan, however, the less common term *bricolage* seems a more apt choice. Employed in the mid-twentieth century by anthropologists, the word described the African tribal practice of making objects for ritual and daily use by combining whatever materials were at hand—shells, nails, wood, even machine parts. The word quickly crossed over into the fine arts, and finally into the decorative arts as well. It applies perfectly to Amelia's innate ability to mix the formal and the informal, fine art and found objects, to create juxtapositions that are not only beautiful and intriguing, but also rich in social history.

Take, for example, the simple West Indian blanket chest standing between a pair of tall windows in the front parlor of the interior designer's Charleston home. Originally intended to hold out-of-season woolens in a nineteenth-century Caribbean household, the chest now supports a neoclassical Italian wall cabinet packed with shells, leather-bound books, an alligator head, Buddha effigies, classical figures, and modern sculpture. "I needed a place for all the objects I'm always picking up," explains Amelia, whose collecting habit ranges from bits of bark, shells, and rocks to centuries-old embroidered textiles, Southern art, and European furniture.

Such juxtapositions, while seeming modern at first glance, can be traced back to early Southern life, when new residents of Charleston, fresh from England or Barbados, created makeshift households. Combining the few fine furnishings they were able to import with rustic household items cobbled together from local materials, these colonists and their African slaves performed New World bricolage. As urban life in the South became more settled, the decoration of the wealthier homes became more

uniformly English in style and polished in nature. But that early mixture of the rustic and refined continued in plantation households, where mounted hunting trophies, turtle shells, homemade furniture, and forged iron pieces shared space with imported textiles, fine furnishings, and delicate tableware.

Amelia grew up in just such a setting, on a plantation near Charleston owned by her family since the eighteenth century. The designer remembers long afternoons spent wandering the fields and woods, where she collected objects and learned lessons about color, texture, and light that served her later in life. She also gained an understanding of Southern hospitality, whether served up in relaxed kitchens, formal dining rooms, or on breezy porches. In the houses she designs for clients across the country, Amelia now brings all these elements together to create rooms that function beautifully for gatherings of family and friends, with fine antiques and furnishings from around the world, arresting artwork, unexpected *objets*, and colors drawn from nature's infinite palette.

When Amelia first decorated the 1820s Charleston house she has inhabited for fifteen years, she chose a color scheme of warm beiges and gold against which she arranged a collection of Southern and European antiques. Recently, the decorator found she wanted more color in the house, so she revved it up with ravishing shades of saffron, rose, and amber. While she loves many of the furnishings she already possessed, Amelia began bringing West Indian antiques into the mix. "I started

The glowing colors Amelia selected create a pleasing layering effect when the dining room and center hall are viewed through the doorway of the living room. In addition to two unmatched armchairs, the central seating area also includes two modern armless chairs. "You can sit sideways in those, if you prefer," says Amelia, whose goal was to create a comfortable conversation area.

collecting them five or six years ago because they are so in sync with the Southern pieces I already have," she explains. To this worldly range of cultures, Amelia has also been adding more and more elements from the East.

While the Buddhist statues she now favors were uncommon, to say the least, in eighteenth- and nineteenth-century Charleston drawing rooms, there is a long-standing Southern tradition of decorating with items made in China. Entire boatloads of blue-and-white Chinese export ware came into Charleston's harbor, as did smaller shipments of hand-painted textiles and armorial services created for fine Anglo-Colonial homes. A trio of colorful sixteenth-century Thai bowls around which fingers of coral have grown is one of Amelia's favorite objects. Discovered during a nineteenth-century excavation of a wrecked British vessel, the artifact resurfaced recently at the Charleston International Antiques Show.

"I fell in love with everything about it," says Amelia, "the mix of natural and man-made textures; the colors; the fact that it sat on the bottom of the sea for two centuries." The piece now stands on a small table in Amelia's dining room, beneath an Italian folk painting depicting a song bird and a split watermelon. Deep rose-tinted walls resonate with the pink tones of the antique Thai bowls and the Italian paintings to create an ambient backdrop for the room's wood furnishings. These include an antique Indonesian table surrounded by elegant West Indian chairs, circa 1820, of dark mahogany. For curtains, Amelia opted for simple panels of sheer, cream-colored wool, edged with metal-thread trim. Reminiscent of the severe neoclassical window treatments popular in Regency England, the curtains appear at once traditional and modern.

In the living room across the center hall, Amelia plays the same games with color, texture, and style. With four unmatched chairs arrayed around a marble-topped pedestal table, an English mid-eighteenth-century sofa, and several daybeds, the room comfortably seats from four to fourteen people. Modern art hangs on walls illumined by a Regency chandelier, and Asian objects, including antique ceramic jars from India and a bronze seated Buddha from Thailand, adorn a neoclassical mantel. Although she does not call herself a Buddhist ("It's such a high thing to aspire to," she explains.), Amelia has placed Buddhist statues throughout the house as a reminder to keep practicing.

A vibrant Oushak carpet and deep rose-colored walls and cushions create a warm ambiance in the dining room. A simple gilded pier mirror and pair of windows minimally draped with gold-trimmed wool curtains add soft formality, contrasting with the unembellished Indonesian dining table.

The largest of these, an age-darkened, carved wooden Buddha, presides over the center hall that forms the saffron-colored heart of the house. With an eighteenth-century Italian bench, English Regency chairs, a Belgian chest of drawers, and a collection of Southern portrait and landscape paintings, the contents of this space connect the strands of varied cultures that weave through Amelia's home. A reverence for the past mixed with a subtle sense of humor, a regional sensibility combined with global savvy—these elements create a three-dimensional collage of sophisticated Southern style.

LEFT A pale Agra carpet sets a serene tone for the bedroom, where dreamy details like a scene from the French *Monuments of Paris* wallpaper and a length of eighteenth-century Venetian fabric decorate the walls.

ABOVE Amelia retained the rough brick fireplace of this bathroom, used originally as a kitchen, because she loved the texture and color of the old brick. An early twentieth-century French sunburst, an early nineteenth-century Italian settee, and a Moroccan table lend international flair to the space.

155

Love of the *New*

Wealthy Southerners of the eighteenth and nineteenth centuries were enthusiastically modern, ever eager to keep abreast of the hottest styles back home in their mother countries. Whether copying the newest designs of Thomas Chippendale and the Adam brothers or decorating their homes with elegant London silver or chic French *Récamier* sofas, they were utterly à la mode. Many of the homes they built followed shifting architectural styles in England, from the stately handsomeness of Georgian manors to the graceful elegance of Adamesque houses. Within these colonial American houses, rooms were adorned with the same decorative cornice moldings, composition mantel decorations, wood-blocked wallpaper, and chintz upholstery found in the finest London and European residences.

Such modishness continued among the South's upper echelon of wealth until the Civil War, when the region's trade ties with England and Europe were severed and its resources strained. In the aftermath of the war, some cities languished, including Charleston and Natchez, their economies never recovering. There, citizens clung to vestiges of their former opulence. But other cities, among these Savannah and New Orleans, flourished after the war. Residents of these fortunate places once again embraced the new, building bold Richardsonian Romanesque mansions and fanciful Queen Anne houses furnished with weighty Second Empire sofas bought from northeastern fashion capitals and eclectic accoutrements from around the world.

By the early twentieth century, well-to-do Southerners in Atlanta, Nashville, Memphis, and elsewhere were embracing the Colonial Revival—a new style that looked to old sources for inspiration. The Georgian houses of Williamsburg, the *maisons de famille* of provincial France, the half-timbered cottages of the English Cotswolds, the stuccoed farmhouses of Spain—these became the models for modern homes in the region's first suburbs. Today, the Colonial Revival is once more all the rage, and many modern-day Southerners are building houses inspired by traditional styles. Other contemporary Southerners are dwelling in thoroughly modern structures inspired by the spare simplicity of Mies van der Rohe and Le Corbusier, yet still bearing venerable Southern hallmarks such as white columns and porches. Together, these homeowners reveal the paradox at the heart of Southern style: no matter how new something may look, it is still somehow centered in the past. And no matter how old something appears, it still speaks of the South's enduring love of the new.

In Michele Seiver's Colonial Revival living room, a Le Corbusier chrome-and-leather lounge demonstrates a modern approach to design. But antique garden statuary and a Niermann Weeks chandelier glimpsed in the garden room beyond suggest that a softer, more feminine aesthetic is also at work.

Palladio by the Beach

HOUSE OF REBECCA AND ROY ANDERSON: GULFPORT, MISSISSIPPI

The sunburst-patterned limestone floor and art deco-inspired railing in Rebecca and Roy Anderson's stair hall offer a modern interpretation of the Old World tradition of grand spiral staircases. The minimalist door treatments and almost ironically elegant accoutrements add further contemporary style to the space.

When Rebecca and Roy Anderson asked Louisiana-based architect Ken Tate to design a house on the Gulf shore of Mississippi, Ken envisioned an unlikely pairing of styles: Andrea Palladio's sixteenth-century Italian villas and the Creole plantations of Louisiana and the Caribbean. "I tried to create something that looked as if Palladio had been sent to the Gulf Coast to design a house—channeling him through the climate and the Creole vernacular," says Ken, a classical architect with a penchant for the vernacular. Neither purely Palladian nor perfectly Creole, the resulting design is a dynamic fusion of both. Destroyed in 2005 by Hurricane Katrina, the house is now as much a part of the past as the structures that inspired it.

Classical elements including columns, entablatures, and cornices ornamented the facade, arranged beneath a hipped roof clad in slate. A distinguishing characteristic of French colonial plantations in the Caribbean and Louisiana territory (which included this part of Mississippi), this style of roof was originally favored for functional purposes. Ideal for drawing hot air up and out of lower rooms, the broad, apron-shaped roof accommodated extra storage and, in some instances, extra bedroom space. Ken employed the form in the Andersons' house not only for its historical associations, but also because it created a dynamic geometry for the compound, which included a two-story central block surrounded by four one-story pavilions, each capped with a pyramidal roof. "We loved the way the different shapes of house looked from the beach," Rebecca remembers. "It was like a wonderful sand castle."

When he was designing the plan, Ken drew inspiration from plantations of Martinique and St. Barts, where outbuildings with a variety of functions were arranged around the main house. Although these Caribbean plantations were quite primitive, the architect applied Palladian symmetry and refinement to create the Andersons' elegant house. The pavilion standing to the left of the beachside facade, for example, served as a guest bedroom with the breezy atmosphere of a sleeping porch, while the one to the right was an open-air dining room. A deep porch running across the facade

The easy flow among open,
enclosed, and semi-enclosed
spaces of the house reflects
Creole tradition designed to
allow residents to enjoy—or
avoid—the effects of seaborne
breezes, rain, and bright
coastal light. While continental
European houses utilized
solid shutters, colonists in
tropical climates preferred
louvered shutters like these,
which permit ventilation
while filtering the sunlight
and deflecting rain.

LEFT Interior designers Ann Tully and Bert Brown selected this gold-leaf wallpaper by Roger Arlington for the stair hall ceiling. In contrast to the understated elegance of Ken's architecture, the designers introduced more overtly luxurious and glamorous effects balanced by simpler forms and natural textures.

RIGHT In the family living room, crown moldings, a carved stone mantel, and French doors with the gently curving outline of segmental arches create a dignified setting for more whimsical furnishings. Giorgetti armchairs upholstered in a bold checkerboard pattern create high-voltage visual verve when set upon a striped Scandinavian carpet.

connected the two, providing a fluid circulation pattern that invited residents and their guests to move easily among interior and exterior spaces. Two more pavilions bracketed the rear facade, one housing a master bedroom suite and the other a breakfast room. A loggia facing the pool behind the house joined the two pavilions, allowing the Andersons to travel from one side of the house to the other through an open-air passageway.

This easy flow among open, enclosed, and semi-enclosed spaces was common in Creole architecture, in which interior halls were rare. In Creole colonial plantations (and urban residences, as well), many rooms had French doors opening onto porches that functioned as exterior hallways connecting interior rooms. Porches also served, at times, as exterior rooms for gathering, dining, and sleeping. Further blurring the boundaries between indoor and outdoor spaces, louvered shutters were typically used in place of solid doors, rendering the exterior walls of Creole houses practically transparent. In the Andersons' house, louvered shutters and blinds were employed throughout, deflecting the sun and creating a dynamic zigzag pattern of light and shadow on walls and floors.

Although Ken consciously evoked these Creole traditions while designing the Andersons' house, he discovered later that another, forgotten prototype was also guiding him. "Several years after finishing the Andersons' house, I came across a drawing of Kingsley Plantation," says the architect, referring to a late eighteenth-century colonial plantation in Florida built by John McQueen. The drawing was published in a book entitled *Florida's Colonial Architectural Heritage*, in which Kingsley Plantation's form—a rectangle surrounded by four square pavilions—was likened to a design by Sebastio Serlio. A contemporary of Palladio, Serlio published his design in a sixteenth-century volume entitled *The Five Books of Architecture*, which was a well-known source of inspiration for Georgian English architecture. "When I discovered the book again and looked at the drawings, I realized that this form must be an archetype," says Ken.

LEFT In the master bedroom, severe elements including the plain, louvered French windows and the bed's iron canopy invoke the simple styles found in Creole plantations. But luxurious details, including the Italian chandelier, circa 1790, and the French art deco chair, create pleasingly sensual anachronisms.

RIGHT Contemporary Italian chairs designed by Giorgetti and sconces inspired by Giacometti contribute a stylishly minimalist vignette in a hallway. Paintings by Donald Tully add further notes of sensual minimalism to the space.

In keeping with the fluid arrangement of rooms present in Kingsley Plantation and its Serlian prototype, the first-floor entertaining rooms of the Andersons' house flowed directly into one another without benefit of hallways. Wide openings with elegant door surrounds connect the spaces, and shifts in the pattern of the floor's limestone parquet marked the transitions from room to room. Many of the interior's architectural details—wood paneled walls, stone mantels, coved ceilings—were traditional in appearance. But the open floor plan, monochromatic palette, and modern flourishes, including the art deco glamour of the spiral staircase in the entrance hall, created a contemporary atmosphere.

"We wanted our house to be furnished with beautiful French antiques, which are so often found in this part of the South, mixed with contemporary pieces," Rebecca said. New Orleans–based interior designers Ann Tully and Bert Brown forged a perfect balance by mixing European antiques, custom-made pieces, and contemporary Italian furniture throughout the entertaining rooms. In the dining room, for example, chairs designed in the Louis XV style by Tully and Brown surrounded a French Empire dining table. Tall, slender console tables with a modern aspect, also a Tully and Brown design, added a contemporary note to the room, as did paintings of fruit by Southern artist Maggie

Hasbrouck. While the ceiling's gold leaf wallpaper by Roger Arlington and Louis Philippe sconces and chandelier created an air of refined formality, a woven grass carpet contributed a casual, seaside touch.

A more modern mood pervaded the family sitting room, where a striped Scandinavian rug and contemporary Italian chairs by Giorgetti created strong graphic highlights. A square metal and glass table designed by Holly Hunt echoed the linear modernity of the striped carpet, and bronze sconces inspired by the sculpture of Giacometti brought an irregular, hand-wrought element into the room. In the bedrooms, however, Tully and Brown explored the sensual, romantic aspect of French West Indies style. In the master bedroom, a wrought-iron bed with diaphanous draperies shared space with a delicate gilt and crystal chandelier, circa 1790, and a French art deco chair. In the guest room, gauzy curtains fluttered over French doors and louvered blinds created shadows as the sun moved around the beachside pavilion.

While the house faced the gulf, its rear facade opened onto a large courtyard filled with a pool that offered cool repose. An outbuilding stood across the pool's shimmering waters, with a simple columned porch crowned by a hipped roof echoing that of the house. Covered with pale lime-tinted stucco and crowned with slate in shades of lavender, blue, and gray, the outbuilding, like the house, reflected the mercurial Gulf Coast light. "At the end of a stormy day, the light-refracting qualities of the materials made the house luminous in the waning light," Ken wrote before Hurricane Katrina. Years after the storm destroyed her home, Rebecca remarks, "It will live forever in our minds as a beautiful villa by the sea."

LEFT Skilled Mexican artisans carved the limestone fountainheads reminiscent of ancient Mexican sculpture. "These meshed nicely with the area's brief history as an outpost of the Spanish Caribbean," Ken notes.

RIGHT The hipped roof and spare symmetry of the pool house create, in miniature, the silhouette of typical Creole plantation houses. The masonry and stucco hood over the outdoor grill are suggestive of an old French kitchen's chimney breast.

Vivid Revival

HOUSE OF MICHELE SEIVER: SPRING VALLEY, DISTRICT OF COLUMBIA

When Michele Seiver first came to Washington, D.C., to work for the senator from her native state of Wyoming, she thought that she would soon return home. But instead, she remained to join the city's closely knit community of expatriates. When she and her husband bought their first home, she enthusiastically adopted the traditional style favored by Old Guard Washington. "Chintz, a down-filled sofa that took a half hour to get out of, silver, Limoges figurines, an extensive collection of English Staffordshire pieces," is how she describes the decor. Fifteen years later, she was newly divorced and ready for a change. "I woke up one day and decided 'I'm over all this stuff,' and sold it at auction," she remembers.

The proceeds from the auction allowed her to buy a new home and decorate it in luxurious contemporary style. "I'm not sure I believe in destiny," she says, "but I do know that for years I walked by a broken-down house on a hill in Spring Valley and knew I would one day live there." The house was built by the Catholic Archdiocese of Washington as the archdeacon's residence. Designed in the stately Georgian style favored during the Colonial Revival of the mid-twentieth century, it boasted a magnificent entrance hall with black-and-white marble parquet, a spiral staircase, and an interior fountain.

When the archdiocese decided the house was too ostentatious for clerical purposes, it became home to a couple who lived there for thirty years. By the time Michele discovered it, the house had fallen into disrepair, inhabited only by the aging widow and her nurse, both of whom lived in just a few rooms. "The porch tilted, peeling paint fell like rain from the shutters, and overgrown shrubs covered the grounds," Michele recalls. When the widow died, Michele made an offer to the estate, having only seen one peek of the interior. "I peered into the front door and saw an enormous crystal chandelier presiding over the well-worn marble floor and a dried-up fountain," she says. Once she purchased the house, she discovered a dilapidated interior with faded wallpaper and bare bulbs hanging in the rooms.

At once Michele began the process of renovation, retaining many original details, including elegant moldings and plaster ceiling medallions, but taking down walls to create larger rooms, removing doors, and widening entranceways for better flow. Despite her renovation crew's protests, she had them jackhammer the entrance hall's marble floor, replacing it with a modern pavement of broken limestone. She had light-colored wood floors stained espresso brown and ceilings equipped with recessed lighting. "It's amazing how much modern lighting updates the look of a room," Michele comments.

The remodeled and redecorated house now gives an impression of harmonious balance between the past and the present. While the gracefully curving staircase appears traditional, the irregular limestone paving, a carpet runner cut into the shape of a fleur-de-lis, and a vintage Le Corbusier lounge visible from the entrance hall are modern in style. Two antique stone urns, mottled with patina, support a slab of Corian that serves as a console table in the hall. A cast-stone bust of the ancient beauty Helen of Troy sits on the table, bejeweled with a faux pearl necklace. This playful blending of the old and

While the mood of the foyer is one of light-hearted elegance, Michele injects high-voltage energy in her office with espresso-colored pleather curtains, a bold zebra-inspired carpet, and a Holly Hunt X-table.

LEFT Michele replaced the living room's original neoclassical mantel with a much bolder mica fireplace that anchors the long room. While the ceiling medallion and the Georgian style moldings recall the past, contemporary furniture in a palette of black-and-white creates a contemporary atmosphere.

OVERLEAF In the house's square dining room, Michele decided to bring in circular forms to create a more dynamic energy. A round sea-grass rug, a circular slab of limestone for the tabletop, large mix-media panels with a gilded circle and square, and the graceful curves of a Niermann Weeks chandelier all balance the room's right angles.

the new, in which a timeless sense of beauty trumps tradition, is the spirit that fuels Michele's approach to decorating.

Her office, opening just off the foyer, is a perfect example. Bookcases embellished with dentil moldings and Corinthian pilasters establish a classical setting against which Michele set an abstract zebra-patterned area rug and dark chocolate pleather curtains. "When you add the zebra and the plastic curtains, then it's easier to live with the old-fashioned look," she explains. In the living room, Michele retained the ceiling medallion, but removed a Federal-style mantel that was out of sync with her modern vision. She replaced it with a boldly geometric mica fireplace surmounted by a large round mirror that recalls the bull's-eye mirrors favored in homes of the 1700s.

In the sunroom, formerly a screened porch, Michele created a garden theme using a large urn as the base for a stone deer—an antique garden statue that once belonged to the du Pont family. A collection of botanical prints she brought from her previous residence hang on the walls in a montage style that lends them a fresh, modern look. Contemporary white love seats arranged in a semicircle around the table add a modern counterpoint to the more traditional Niermann Weeks chandelier that graces the room.

While the garden room's many windows create a sense of space and light, the dining room, solely illuminated by a bay window, felt dark and enclosed. To counteract this, Michele decorated the room in shades of white, cream, and gold that reflect the light and visually enlarge the space. After considering expensive ostrich-skin-style wallpaper, she hired Washington-based decorative painter Teresa Saathoff to create a customized faux finish on the walls. Painted with randomly spaced opalescent dots, the pattern mimics the real ostrich-skin upholstery on the dining room chairs.

In the kitchen next door, Michele removed a mudroom to create a light-filled corner where she stenciled the names of French desserts—including her daughter Madeleine's name—on a chocolate brown background. To balance the kitchen's conservative cabinets, she hung an oversize linen and aluminum pendant light over a copper dining table. In her bedroom, she created the same balance of old and new with a heavily draped canopy bed juxtaposed with a bold Holly Hunt table and a modern Italian swivel chair.

Although at first it might seem hard to reconcile this modern design aesthetic with a historically-based architectural style, a look at the history of the Colonial Revival suggests otherwise. The style first arose after the Centennial Exposition of 1876, when Americans regained interest in the Georgian and Federal architecture of their founding fathers. Some Americans built faithful reproductions of early prototypes, but others simply integrated aspects of colonial styles into then-popular Queen Anne and Shingle-style houses.

A second Colonial Revival occurred in the 1930s, following the development of Colonial Williamsburg as a major history-based public attraction. As in the past, some people religiously re-created the proportions and architectural details of early American styles. But in general, the spirit was that of reinterpretation, of merging classical decorative details into houses with a more modern approach to material, scale, and room use. "When you add a modern mantel or a piece of contemporary furniture, suddenly these old-fashioned rooms look hip," says Michele.

In the kitchen, a distressed copper table creates an informal dining area for Michele and her three children, Sam, Jack, and Madeleine. Madeleine's name is among the list of French desserts Michele had painted upon a chocolate-colored wall.

Gun Metal and Roses

HOUSE OF DEBRA AND JERRY SHRIVER: NEW ORLEANS, LOUISIANA

Taffeta draperies, raffia blinds, matte linen, and silk velvet upholstery create a sensual setting in Debra and Jerry Shriver's living room in the French Quarter of New Orleans. Luminous Lucite tables with the unexpected detail of Moorish arches contrast with the lichen-like texture of stone urns and the shimmering surface of a painting by Patrick Pietropoli.

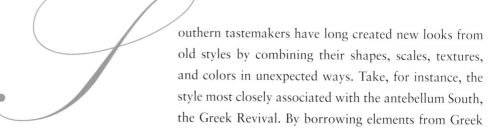

*S*outhern tastemakers have long created new looks from old styles by combining their shapes, scales, textures, and colors in unexpected ways. Take, for instance, the style most closely associated with the antebellum South, the Greek Revival. By borrowing elements from Greek temples and isolating and rearranging them, alternately simplifying or embellishing them, Southern architects invented a fresh style that was intensely popular throughout much of the nineteenth century. With its bold scale and unabashed decorative bravado, the style is clearly distinguished from the preceding Federal and Georgian fashions while still drawing from the same basic set of classical influences.

The same can be said of the New Orleans home of Debra and Jerry Shriver. A Greek Revival townhouse filled with French and Gustavian antiques, the residence creates a distinctly contemporary impression thanks to unexpected juxtapositions of color, texture, artwork, and decorative accoutrements. "I like putting straw next to silk, linen next to velvet, and mixing metal tones: gold, silver, bronze, brass, pewter, and mercury-backed glass," says Debra, who collects eighteenth-century French furniture and contemporary photography with equal passion.

"I see Debra as a very modern person coming from a very old, traditional world," says Hal Williamson, the Shrivers' New Orleans–based interior designer. Like Debra, who is a high-powered media executive at Hearst Corporation in New York, Hal also has family ties to Alabama. "As Southerners, we love our things, and the romance and beauty of the past," he explains. "Debra and I wanted to capture all of that, but also to create an interior that is beautiful and glamorous, and that has a definite modern edge."

"In the past," says Debra, "when I decorated a house, I would bring in a certain period and decorate the whole house to that period. Here, we have my photography collection mixed with Louis XV, Louis XVI, Louis Philippe, and Gustavian-style pieces." On the ground floor, these are arranged in a pair of entertaining rooms decorated in a tone-on-tone palette that looks at first to be quite modern. But Debra points out that the

inspiration for the color scheme came in part from the ancient East, where greens and blues, plums and purples, reds and pinks are often combined in the decorative arts.

To illustrate her point, she indicates two oversize photographs by Laura McPhee of antique dwellings in India decorated in time-faded shades of blue, pink, and violet. One depicts an abandoned living room with peeling paint and damaged ancestral portraits; the other, a sun-faded courtyard. "I'm drawn to decay," says Debra, whose collection also includes photographs of overblown flowers, Southern architecture, and statuary in varying states of romantic decadence. "It's just part of being a Southerner," she explains. "We are very comfortable with old things, but we like new things, too."

Like most French Quarter townhouses, the Shrivers' has a pair of entertaining rooms paralleled by a hallway running from the front door to a back courtyard. Debra and Jerry, who writes about food and wine, love to entertain, so part of Hal's goal was to design spaces that could function well for both large parties and small dinners. To this end, the designer unified the front parlor with the dining room behind it by selecting paint colors in related tones: amethyst with a little taupe added to it for the parlor and deeper plum for the dining room.

In the living room, opulent cascades of silk in a shade of lavender with pewter tones fall from iron drapery poles mounted above two tall windows. "When people think of New Orleans, they think of ball gowns," says Hal. "I wanted to create a ball-gown–style drapery with a modern edge for this house." He achieved the look by gathering the fabric into bustle-like knots at the top, then letting it fall straight to the floor. Silk tassel trim by Houlès, a leading Paris designer of passementerie, completes the glamorous effect. Roman shades of woven grass hang behind the curtains, muting the light and contributing an informal, modern texture to the mix.

"Purple on taupe, taupe on gray, gray on silver, silver on glass . . ." are the words Debra uses to describe the palette she and designer Hal Williamson chose for the living room. This muted, nearly monochromatic palette lends an air of luxurious minimalism to the otherwise opulent decor.

LEFT Designed by Roulhac
Toledano for Architextiles,
the linen upholstery covering
these Louis XV chairs features
oversized reproductions of
New Orleans and Louisiana
motifs from antique prints. A
gilt-edged pot-de-crème set
adds luster to the chalkiness of
the Gustavian-style table, and
the silk-screen portrait by
Richard Thomas of Mahalia
Jackson lends a jazzy high
note to the room.

RIGHT The Swedish table
divides into a simple, gate-
legged rectangle and a pair of
half-round table-ends used as
consoles on either side of the
fireplace. A carpet by Barbara
Barry and the lavender ging-
ham Hal chose for the chair
backs add subtly modern notes
to balance the formality of the
antique furnishings.

In a similar study in contrast, Hal selected heavyweight Bergamo linen to cover a Louis XV sofa and soft velvet for wing chairs of the same period. A contemporary coffee table and an occasional table inspired by the French Directoire style offer clean, angular lines that balance the voluptuous curves of the room's older furniture. Even greater minimalism comes in the form of a Himalayan silk carpet with a subtle strié pattern in taupe and gray, which softens and brightens the coffee-colored pine floor. A Louis Philippe mirror with a silvered frame and an Italian chandelier add final gleaming highlights to the room, which shimmers with natural and manmade light.

"I've tried to bring in a lot of light with French and Venetian mirrors, mercury glass, chandeliers, silver gelatin prints, even silk rugs that have a reflective quality," explains Debra. These gleaming elements magnify the limited natural light that comes into the entertaining rooms. With no direct source of light in the dining room, Debra and Hal still

LEFT A French desk with
curvaceous knees, rococo
carvings of shells and bows,
and an original rouge marble
top sets the tone for this
unabashedly feminine corner
overlooking the courtyard.
An image of female strength
and individuality, the large
photograph of Ella Fitzgerald
by Steven Forster adds deeper
character to the pretty room.

RIGHT Captivated by their
brilliant colors, Debra picked
up a handful of silk tassels in
shades of fuchsia, chartreuse,
peacock blue, and violet in a
Paris shop. In toned-down
shades, these colors permeate
the house's decoration.
Grisaille details, including this
painted French chest and
antique Venetian mirror,
complement the lush palette.

succeeded in creating a space that glows with the soft light of a pearl. An eighteenth-
century Swedish dining table stands in the center of the room, its chalky white finish
reflecting the light of the Italian chandelier that hangs above it.

"The table was one of our best finds for the house," says Hal. "With four pieces—a
drop-leaf table, two half-round consoles, and another piece—it can be put together to
span both rooms and seat twenty-four, or assembled with fewer pieces for small parties."
But Hal's greatest enthusiasm is reserved for the toile depicting scenes from New Orleans
and Louisiana history, designed by Roulhac Toledano of Architextiles and printed by
Koessel Studios on Bergamo linen. Each of eight antique French dining room chairs is
upholstered with a different scene.

To prevent the room from looking overly formal, Debra hung a brightly colored silk-
screen portrait of jazz great Mahalia Jackson, by Richard Thomas, over the French
intaglio chest where she stores a collection of gilt-edged Limoges porcelain. Jazz is one of
the things that attracted both Debra and Jerry to New Orleans, which they began

LEFT In the *garçonnière* that parallels a balcony overlooking the courtyard, Hal created an informal sitting room for Debra and Jerry and one or two friends. A segmental map of Paris sets a sophisticated tone, complemented by the caned French sofa below. However, granny-apple green walls, Ikat-style upholstery, and a bright Oushak carpet create a lively mood.

RIGHT Hal suggested another monochromatic palette for the master bedroom, this one a cool blue that offers relief from the heat and urban traffic of the French Quarter streets below. Louis XV bergère armchairs upholstered in a blue-and-cream silk stripe create sedate contrast to the exuberantly embroidered Lee Joffa silk duvet cover.

visiting as a couple twenty-five years ago when they were both working as journalists in Florida. "Three of our passions are music, food, and architecture," says Debra. "That's the holy trinity here in New Orleans."

Although they live in New York and travel the world, Debra and Jerry have kept coming back to New Orleans, despite the devastation of Hurricane Katrina. "We never wavered in our desire to have a home here," says Jerry, who loves the fact that he can sit in the courtyard and hear the sounds of horses' hooves, steamboat whistles, cathedral bells, and a street-hawker selling pies. While the kitchen and mosaic tile bathroom opening onto the courtyard are the most modern rooms in the house, the courtyard, with its glazed Italian pots and French metal folding chairs, feels like a little slice of New Orleans' past.

It is this simultaneity of the old and the new, of the earthy and the ethereal, that continues to weave a spell of enchantment for this worldly couple. Debra recalls coming home one late afternoon when she had accidentally left the door to the courtyard open. "I came into the hallway and I could see the garden in the flicker of gaslight as the sunlight was fading," she says. "I could smell the wet bricks and the moss and the dirt. It was like I had entered a secret garden. I closed the door and I was home."

Attraction of Opposites

AN ART COLLECTOR'S PENTHOUSE: ATLANTA, GEORGIA

Architect Norman Askins designed a graceful curving balcony and round second-story windows to soften the large, open space of this collector's Atlanta penthouse. Interior designer Nancy Braithwaite chose shades of charcoal and gray for the walls, creating a dusky background against which modern and ancient art take the stage.

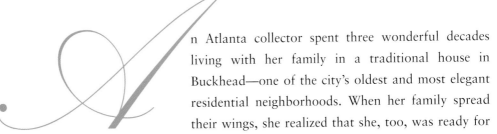

An Atlanta collector spent three wonderful decades living with her family in a traditional house in Buckhead—one of the city's oldest and most elegant residential neighborhoods. When her family spread their wings, she realized that she, too, was ready for a change. "I wanted an adult space that was big enough not only for my art collection, but also for visiting children and grandchildren," she explains. "I also desired plenty of room for all my books, and most especially, I wanted space to entertain." During her search for a new home, she fell in love with a two-story penthouse overlooking a garden in Buckhead. Describing the unfinished space, she says, "It was just a shell, so it sparked many possibilities for me."

The collector dreamed of surrounding herself with her collection of works on paper by modern masters including Willem de Kooning, Jackson Pollack, Pablo Picasso, and Louise Bourgeois. She also looked forward to sharing these works with others. "These drawings expose each artist's hand and intention so clearly," she explains. "They draw the viewer directly into a dialog." Many of the works in her collection are quite large, so they needed space to spread out. Others are small, inviting the viewer to come in for a closer look. All of them are fragile, requiring protection from the sun, yet precisely angled artificial light for viewing.

Creating the perfect setting for these rather demanding works of art was one of several requests that the collector presented to prominent Atlanta-based architect Norman Askins. She envisioned an open floor plan for the penthouse, "so that people can move around with ease, whether at parties or museum tours," she explains. But the homeowner also wanted enclosed, intimate spaces for reading or fireside dinners with friends. Norman's challenge was to create a space that was both modern and traditional, expansive and intimate, full of light, but not too much. The homeowner also asked Atlanta-based interior designer Nancy Braithwaite to join the design team.

The warm stone surround of
the living room fireplace
softens its modern form, and
the engaging carved face of an
ancient Roman stele placed
in a niche above the mantel
enlivens the space with
complex humanity.

LEFT Bookshelves line the passage leading into the library where the resident enjoys occasional quiet meals with friends, as well as reading and correspondence. Askins designed paneling in a traditional style that contrasts with the living room's otherwise unadorned walls to create an intimate, enclosed sense of space.

RIGHT Before creating this modern domicile, the resident and her husband collected French antiques to adorn a more traditional home. In her new penthouse apartment, she retained pieces from the collection, including this eighteenth-century sideboard, above which hangs a watercolor by Francesco Clemente.

The success of the trio's collaboration finds full expression in the soaring living room at the center of the dwelling and the two small rooms that bracket it. Measuring 40 feet wide and two-stories high, the central space could easily have felt overwhelming, losing the human scale the resident desired. To solve the problem, Norman added second-floor balconies that break up the room's volume and contribute engaging architectural details. The balconies also provide gallery-like spaces that accommodate changing exhibitions of the homeowner's collection. Norman also designed round second-story windows to soften the room's rectangular shapes and admit, indirect light. The architect repeated the circular form in a niche above the living room's fireplace, where the collector mounted one of her most recent acquisitions—a third-century B.C. Roman stele with eyes that gaze into the room.

The walls of the living room are painted deep, velvety gray, a sophisticated neutral tone that Nancy chose as the perfect background for the art. "I felt that the art needed room to breathe," says the designer. "Neutrals set backdrops for things more successfully than bright, vibrant colors. I pared everything down to receive the art. The furniture came afterwards." When it was time to place the furniture, Nancy created two seating areas. One is furnished entirely with contemporary upholstered pieces, including sofas just the right size for two or three guests to sit comfortably and chat. A marble-topped coffee table stands between them and a large ottoman sits nearby, ready to be pulled toward either sofa or the table by guests who wish to join a conversation.

Across the long room, a Louis XV table with delicately curving walnut legs stands on a zebra rug, forming the focal point of the second seating area. Two cane-backed French chairs painted black face off across the table, looking both antique and modern

LEFT The resident's collection includes not only modern drawings and watercolors, but also ancient sculptures, including this fragment from an Imperial Roman sarcophagus. Designed as a funerary object, this face of a man gazes gravely through the centuries to address the living.

RIGHT A mysterious self-portrait by Sigmar Polke keeps an eye on this guest room, which also serves as an impromptu dining space when parties overflow the living and dining rooms.

at the same time. "The resident owned a lot of French furniture, and one of the goals was to use as much of it as possible in her new home," Nancy explains. "I painted these reproduction cane-back chairs black to make them seem more contemporary."

Just behind the black French chairs, two openings lead into the dining room. This intimate room's ceiling is one-half the height of the living room, but with two walls of windows, the room still feels expansive. Diaphanous silver draperies soften the light, and light-taming, rolling blinds add yet another level of protection for the room's art-work. Working closely with the collector to create spaces personalized for her cherished possessions, Norman created a wide niche in one wall, where a robustly carved, eigh-teenth-century French sideboard stands. In an anachronistic vignette, a collection of Delft china sits atop the antique piece and an intensely colored watercolor by Clemente hanging above it. "These are all things my husband and I have collected and loved."

On the other side of the living room, Norman and Nancy created another intimate-ly proportioned room that became a library for the resident's large collection of books. In order to create a cozy atmosphere for reading and reflecting, Norman designed milled wood paneling and interior shutters. These details contribute a traditional, architecton-ic appearance that contrasts with the living room's more contemporary style. "One of the main ideas of the design was to create a warm, human scale in what is a large, mod-ern setting," Norman explains.

Built-in bookshelves hold volumes about art, history, and politics, and comfortable upholstered pieces cluster around a fireplace with an antique mantel the resident brought from her previous home. An eighteenth-century French card table and chairs sit before a window looking out over the treetops and sky. "Sometimes when I entertain, we sit at this table and enjoy the view," she says. "When I'm alone, the sofa is a com-fortable place to read across from the fireplace." But the homeowner is never really alone in this room or elsewhere in the apartment, thanks to the human spirit of the art surrounding her. In the library, for instance, a luminous marble fragment of an Imperial Roman sarcophagus depicts the head of a young man with soft lips, curling hair, and soulful eyes that speak eloquently of ancient times.

While taming bright natural light was a challenge in these rooms, the apartment's foyer posed quite a different problem. Located in the building's core, the room had almost no natural light—a factor Norman and Nancy transformed into an advantage. Employing shades of charcoal gray and black plum, Nancy established a shadowy palette that creates a moment of repose before the foyer opens into brighter, airier spaces. To contribute a sculptural touch, Norman designed a sinuous iron railing to decorate the spiral staircase. The homeowner added the final element: fine art from her collection including an energetic sketch by de Kooning and a meltingly curvaceous bronze figure of a woman by Gaston Lachaise. "The serenity of the apartment and the intensity of the art are in perfect balance," commented a visitor after completing a tour with the Smithsonian American Art Museum. "That was exactly what I had in mind," replied the collector.

Moon River House

HOUSE OF LOUISE AND SCOTT LAURETTI: SKIDAWAY ISLAND, GEORGIA

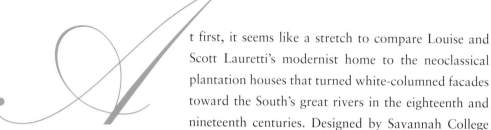

Savannah College of Art and Design professor, architect Tim Woods, describes the white columns extending from the facade of Louise and Scott Lauretti's house as legs or buttresses. Inspired by the work of modernist icon Mies van der Rohe, they reach out gracefully to delineate an exterior room—part porch, part terrace.

At first, it seems like a stretch to compare Louise and Scott Lauretti's modernist home to the neoclassical plantation houses that turned white-columned facades toward the South's great rivers in the eighteenth and nineteenth centuries. Designed by Savannah College of Art and Design professor and architect Tim Woods, the Laurettis' house is mostly modern in its materials, including steel beams, plate glass, powder-coated aluminum, industrial plastic, and stained concrete. There is a fair amount of travertine paving the large living area's floor and parts of the terraces on the first and second floors. But this is the only Old World material used in the dwelling, which owes more to Mies van der Rohe than to the ancient Greek and Roman prototypes that monopolize the architecture of the Old South.

However, if you approach the house from the creek that runs behind it, the similarities to Old South architecture become more evident. Tall, slender, off-white columns extend like spider legs from the house to create a graceful colonnade spanning the creekside facade. These frame a series of stone-and-concrete terraces that rise gently from the level of the creek to a porch and, finally, to the entrance of the house. This progression from low-lying land to porch to parlor is identical to the plan of many antique plantation houses. So is the Laurettis' decision to have the primary facade of the house oriented to the water (and the best view) instead of the street.

"We bought this piece of land because it has a 270-degree view of the landscape," says Scott. "I wanted to use as much of the outside as possible in the design of the house." While many of the other houses in The Landings, a sea island development outside of Savannah, tended to turn their main facades to the street, the Laurettis wanted their house to focus on the landscape. "Most Americans orient their houses so that the most obvious physical features are evident to the person on the sidewalk," he continued. "I'm not that concerned about the person on the sidewalk."

When Scott first met with Tim, he brought photographs of houses in the seaside villages of Greece. "The houses there are white, vertical, linear structures that face the sea," he comments. In addition to asking his architect to consider the orientation and geometric rhythms of Greek island architecture, Scott also put historic allusions aside. "I like an open, modern house," he told him. And that is what the architect designed while keeping in mind the various historical allusions that applied.

"The idea of making an uninterrupted visual connection between the inside and the outside was very important," says Tim. To achieve this goal, he used thin steel columns to support the high ceiling of an open living space on the first floor. Arrayed along the walls of the 30 by 30-foot room, these columns frame plate glass windows that capture scenes of the ever-changing coastal landscape and sky beyond. Louvered sunshades made of powder-coated aluminum hang above the windows. With serrated blades positioned at a 35-degree angle, they let in the minimum amount of sunlight during summer and the maximum light in winter.

"The shades mitigate the bright light and heat without blocking the view," Tim explains, likening them to the louvered shutters and blinds favored in the antebellum South. They also create a decorative effect, casting dappled shadows on the room's travertine marble floor that imitate that of the moss-draped oaks. "The way the light plays with the forms of the house was very important to me," adds the architect, who specializes in designing modern houses that function naturally, beautifully, and efficiently in the South's coastal climate.

Tim selected travertine flooring for the living room for its gentle reflective quality, but he chose a much more modern material for the walls that separate the large space from adjacent rooms. Panels of extruded plastic and powder-coated aluminum form translucent, moveable walls delineating two small rooms, which serve as Louise's office and a guest room/office space. The translucent plastic allows natural light from the living room to illuminate these rooms by day, and at night, when the lights inside the rooms are turned on, a soft, warm glow emanates from the screen-like walls.

The same materials create a set of screens delineating the kitchen from the living area beyond. The Laurettis, who use the space both for family dining and large entertainments, enjoy the flexibility the arrangement allows. The kitchen island is usually reserved for family dining, and the entire living area is quite frequently used for big parties. "If you're having people over and you're cooking, you can open up the screens and use this as a service area," says Louise, indicating the kitchen's stainless steel island.

Although they frequently entertain, the Laurettis' primary concern was to create a comfortable home for themselves and their two young daughters, Sofia and Gabbi. When the family is not enjoying the ground-floor rooms together, they can be found on the second floor, where bedrooms and upstairs terraces provide tree-house-like hideaways. This floor is attained by climbing a transparent staircase that seems to float in space, thanks to open treads that allow the light and surrounding views to pass right through.

The exterior columns create long shadows that stretch across the travertine marble floor of the large living space. An open-tread staircase and cantilevered travertine fire pit built into the living room's low wall provide a focal point for the large, open space. A venting chimney floats above the fire pit, hanging from the ceiling.

"In a lot of houses, the staircases block the view," says Tim. "In this house, they actually help you see the view." Rising through the living space, the staircase ends in a second-floor hallway with walls of glass framing views of outstretched oak limbs, water, and sky. "The whole house has a transparent core that allows you to see through it," says Scott. "You can see out from anyplace inside it, and you can see in from any-place outside."

Illuminated at twilight, the dynamic facade of the house simultaneously projects into the surrounding setting and recedes into the large glowing space at its center.

203

Acknowledgments

These beautiful images and engaging stories of Southern cosmopolitans could not have come together in this volume without the encouragement, assistance, and generosity of many people. First and foremost, I extend heartfelt thanks to Charles Miers, Publisher of Rizzoli International Publications, for his continued support of my passion for Southern style. Thanks also go to my editor, Sandy Gilbert Freidus, whose guidance and perfectionism are invaluable to creating a flawless final product. Credit for this also goes to the book's copyeditor, Elizabeth Smith. Finally, boundless gratitude goes to my graphic designer, Eric Mueller of Element Group, whose eye for beauty, sophistication, and whimsy I depend upon. I also extend gratitude to Graciela Cattarossi, photographer of my portrait; Gordon Beall, Dick Bibb, and Mick Hales, photographers of the Andersons' house; and Wayne Moore, photographer of the Laurettis' house.

The homeowners who shared their houses, helping me define the concept of the Southern cosmopolitan, are the heart and soul of this book. Many, many thanks to:

Morgan D. Delaney and Osborne Phinizy Mackie of Alexandria
Thomas Jayne and Rick Ellis of New York and New Orleans
Hal Williamson and Dale LeBlanc of New Orleans and Natchez
Joane and Norman Askins of Atlanta
Sarah, Prescott, Lander, and Hayden Dunbar of New Orleans
Susan and Trenholm Walker of Charleston
Quinn Peeper and Michael Harold of New Orleans
Ann and Tim Koerner of New Orleans
Tom Leddy of New York and Savannah
Ann and David Silliman of Charleston
Amelia Handegan of Charleston
Michele Seiver of Spring Valley, District of Columbia
Debra and Jerry Shriver of New York and New Orleans
Rebecca and Roy Anderson of Gulfport, Mississippi
Louise and Scott Lauretti of Skidaway Island, Georgia

Finally, I wish to thank all those who gave me hospitality and/or moral support during this challenging project, including Ellen Kiser and Deborah Wright in Charleston, Celia Dunn in Savannah, John and Elizabeth Ryan in Chapel Hill, my beloved and patient husband Thomas Sully and faithful poodle Jesse, Nancy Ryan and Carrie Portis in Berkeley, and Dr. Antonio Bird and Zoe Hoyle in Asheville. You saved the day more times than I can count.

A French bust of Helen of Troy, adorned by Michele Seiver with faux pearls and a delicate crown, graces the entrance hall of her District of Columbia-area Colonial Revival house.

Resource *Guide*

The following is contact information for the architects, interior designers, decorators, and antiques dealers whose homes are featured this book, in order of their appearance.

THOMAS JAYNE
Thomas Jayne Studio
524 Broadway, Suite 605
New York, New York
212.838.9080
www.thomasjaynestudio.com

HAL WILLIAMSON
Williamson Designs
3646 Magazine Street
New Orleans, Louisiana
504.899.4945
www.williamsondesigns.net

NORMAN ASKINS
Norman Davenport Askins Architect
2995 Lookout Place, NE
Atlanta, Georgia
404.233.6565
www.normanaskins.com

JOANE ASKINS
Atlanta, Georgia
404.814.0517

ROSEMARY JAMES
Faulkner House Designs
624 Pirates Alley
New Orleans, Louisiana
504.586.1609
faulkhouse@aol.com

ANN KOERNER
Ann Koerner Antiques
4021 Magazine Street
New Orleans, Louisiana
504.899.2664
www.annkoerner.com

ANN AND DAVID SILLIMAN
Antiques of the Indies
72 Wentworth Street
Charleston, South Carolina
843.577.6868 or 843.853.2400
www.antiquesoftheindies.com

AMELIA HANDEGAN
Amelia T. Handegan, Inc.
517 King Street, Suite 4
Charleston, South Carolina
843.722.9373
www.athid.com

NANCY BRAITHWAITE
1198 Howell Mill Road, NW, Suite 110
Atlanta, Georgia
404.605.0963

KEN TATE
Ken Tate Architect
P. O. Box 550
Madisonville, Louisiana
985.845.8181
www.kentatearchitect.com

TULLY AND BROWN
Bert Tully, interior designer
504.920.9260
Ann Brown Ross
504.352.6360
ann@anncoxross.com

TIM WOODS, architect
Loci Design Gallery
127 East 54th Street
Savannah, Georgia
912.507.6821
www.locidesigngallery.com

SILKWORKS®
Silkworks Textiles, Inc.
2200 Adeline Street, Suite 140
Oakland, California 94607
510.839.7022
www.silkworkstextiles.com

RIGHT Echoing the soft tones of hydrangea blooms, Old Paris porcelain in an unusual shade of violet combines with oyster plates decorated in bright turquoise. Interior designer Hal Williamson often sets his table using pewter instead of his mother's silver because it creates a slightly less formal appearance.

OVERLEAF Located in the Chinese room of Sarah and Prescott Dunbar's New Orleans house, this Thomas Chippendale chinoiserie over-mantel features moveable carved pagoda bells. "We've arranged Chinese porcelain figurines and jades in the niches, which is what they were originally intended to contain," says Sarah Dunbar.